American Sailor

Other books written by Donald Johnson

Military non-fiction

It Wasn't Just A Job; It Was An Adventure

Christian non-fiction

Faith, Family, Friends

Am I A Good Daddy?

American Sailor

More Adventures To Go With The Job

Donald Johnson

iUniverse, Inc.
New York   Lincoln   Shanghai

American Sailor
More Adventures To Go With The Job

Copyright © 2006 by Donald G Johnson

iUniverse books may be ordered through booksellers or by contacting:

iUniverse
2021 Pine Lake Road, Suite 100
Lincoln, NE 68512
www.iuniverse.com
1-800-Authors (1-800-288-4677)

ISBN-13: 978-0-595-41175-7 (pbk)
ISBN-13: 978-0-595-85531-5 (ebk)
ISBN-10: 0-595-41175-4 (pbk)
ISBN-10: 0-595-85531-8 (ebk)

Printed in the United States of America

With gratitude,

I first dedicate this book to those, who served with me in the U.S. Navy and to all those sailors who have lost their lives in the War on Terrorism for your extraordinary loyalty and service in the protection of this great country we
call the
United States of America.

Contents

Acknowledgements xi

Introduction xiii

Chapter 1—**Ports of Call** 1

    Memories of Subic Bay...By Donald Johnson 2

    The Copyright Pirate Capital of the World...By Donald Johnson 8

    Golf and Mar John...By Donald Johnson 10

    Thai Seafood Pizza...By Donald Johnson 13

    Swan River Wine Cruise...by Donald Johnson 16

    A Japanese Tour...by Donald Johnson 19

    Thank God For COD...By Les Bates 22

Chapter 2—**Navy Humor** 24

    The Secrets of Leadership...By Donald Johnson 25

    Which Service is the Best...Contributed by Donald Johnson 27

    Sailorisms...Contributed by Donald Johnson 28

    Admiral Rickover's Transfer...Contributed by Donald Johnson 29

    A Dog Named Chief...Contributed by Donald Johnson 30

    A Sailor's Promise...Contributed by Donald Johnson 31

    Sailor and Marine...Contributed by Donald Johnson 32

    Almost Perfect...Contributed by Donald Johnson 33

    WARNING to the Family and Friends of a Returning Sailor
    ...Contributed by Donald Johnson 34

    Barracks Inspection...Contributed by Donald Johnson 37

Chapter 3—**Collision At Sea and More** 38

    Collision At Sea...By Les Bates 39

    Where's The Bow Ramp?...By Donald Johnson 41

Chapter 4—World War II Experiences 46

   Uncle Herb Aboard The Makassar Strait…By Donald Johnson 47

   Life Aboard the Sara During WW II…By Vern Bluhm 50

   My Time On Guadalcanal…By Vern Bluhm 68

Chapter 5—Korean War Experiences 70

   Navy Recipients of the Congressional Medal of Honor during the
Korean War…By Donald Johnson 71

Chapter 6—Vietnam Experiences 82

   Looking Back…By Donald Johnson 83

   A Ladder to Heaven…By Donald Johnson 86

   The Forrestal Fire…by Don Cook 91

   Navy Recipients of the Congressional Medal of Honor during the
Vietnam War Era…By Donald Johnson 95

Chapter 7—Middle East Experiences 124

   Tracings in the Sand…By Mark Bell 125

   Flying Around and Over The Persian Gulf…By Donald Johnson 130

Chapter 8—Morals and Ethics 134

   Use of Deadly Force…By Brian Studnicky 135

   Traitors and Polygraphs…By Donald Johnson 144

   Not Recommended for Re-enlistment…By Donald Johnson 148

   Where is Your ID Card?…By Donald Johnson 153

   Decisions, Decisions…By Donald Johnson 156

   More Indy Stories…By Brian Studnicky and Donald Johnson 162

Chapter 9—Special Tributes to the American Sailor 171

   Ode to a Long Lost Shipmate…Contributed by Donald Johnson ..172

   A Man of Integrity…By Donald Johnson 173

   I Was a Sailor Once…Contributed by Donald Johnson 177

   What is a Mustang?…by Donald Johnson 180

Chapter 10—**Patriotic Stories** 182

Our American Symbol...By Donald Johnson 183

I Am Coming!...Contributed by Donald Johnson 185

The Defense of Freedom ...By Donald Johnson 187

A Deck of Cards...Contributed by Donald Johnson 191

When a Soldier Dies...By Jim Willis 193

Acknowledgements

I thank you, Vern Bluhm, my adopted, late in life, dad. You have been close to me for the past 15 years. You read all of my material before it had gone to the publisher and you gave me ideas or made comments on the stories or chapters. I have tried to listen to everything that you say. Why? Because you have been there and done that. You have been the greatest mentor I have ever had. I thank you for your World War II memoirs. Those stories will a part of your legacy. Thank you, Vern.

I thank all of the other contributors of this book.

Thank you, Les Bates, for your stories. Hopefully, people who read this book will see a different side of shipboard life from a supply type perspective instead of a tweaking radioman's. You are a friend and a true mustang.

I met Les in Sacramento on the job when I was working a contract for Kelly Services evaluating standardized tests for various state school systems. Les and I would sit in the lunchroom during our breaks and talk about Navy things. That is when I asked him to contribute to this book. Les is a retired Lieutenant Commander, limited duty officer, of the Supply Corps and he served part of his career on aircraft carriers like those that I did.

Thank you, Don Cook, for your personal story of the Forrestal fire, a story that was on film for all to see in boot camp after the incident. That fire was a lesson learned for future Navy fire fighters. You are a survivor. I thank God for that, or we would not be able to relive the story with you.

Don offered his story to me via one of the various Internet groups that I frequent. Maybe someday we will meet.

Thank you, Mark Bell, for your Gulf story and how your time over there has caused you medical problems. People need to see that side of the story as well. It is a story that you need to tell.

Mark's story is also available on the Internet. He gave me permission to have it reprinted in this book. Mark, we will meet someday.

Thank you, Brian Studnicky, for your stories from the Indy. You are a man of integrity. It is too bad that you were not able to experience more about Navy life on other ships. I know that you learned a little about life and that has made you a better man. You brought so many memories back to me. We will meet someday at an Indy reunion.

Brian and I met through one of the Internet groups. He offered to tell his story. I accepted and as they say, "The rest is history." That chance meeting has turned into a long time Internet/E-mail friendship. I know that we will meet someday at an Indy reunion.

Thank you, Jim Willis. Your poem is apropos for the last writing in the last chapter of this book. Even though it is about soldiers, all we have to do as sailors is to insert the word sailor for soldier and it would tell the same story.

I met Jim at a veteran's event at the American Legion/VFW hall in McMinnville, Oregon. Jim is the Director of Veteran's Affairs for the state of Oregon. I know that we will meet again.

Thank you, to the unknown authors who wrote many of the stories, poems and humor in this book. Many touched my heart and many made me laugh which is good for the heart.

This book would not have been possible if it were not for all of the above mentioned people. I cannot thank you enough.

May the Lord be with you forever and with those who read this book.

Introduction

This is the sequel to my first book about the Navy titled, *It Wasn't Just A Job; It Was An Adventure*. I received so many favorable comments from the book that I felt a sequel was worth doing. I still had some stories to tell. I also wanted other sailors to tell their stories.

Port calls are the highlight of any deployment overseas. I have written several stories about some of those port calls. I have been very truthful in telling these stories, especially about what I did overseas. I am not proud of some of the things that I did. I am a born-again Christian, and now look back on those experiences and wonder why I did what I did. A former co-worker and fellow Mustang officer, Les Bates, who served aboard USS Ranger (CV-64), one of the sister ships to USS Independence (CV-62) that I served aboard, tells about problems that could arise prior to pulling into a great shopping and sightseeing port.

Humor is needed in all aspects of life. I have included several humorous stories and jokes that have floated around the Internet for years. I hope that you will enjoy them.

Shipboard duty is dangerous. Inattention to detail and failure to listen to those who have a bird's eye view of what is going on can result in collisions at sea and a loss of shipboard assets. You will read two stories about at sea incidents that could have turned out to be more tragic than they were. Included in this chapter is a story told by Les Bates about the USS Ranger's collision at-sea, and I have a story about the USS Peoria's loss of her bow ramp off the coast of Japan that injured six sailors, one seriously.

The "Greatest Generation" fought World War II. I have written a story about my mother's oldest brother, Herb McElroy, who served onboard the USS Makassar Strait (CVE-91) that provided planes and pilots for Combat Air Patrol during the Battle of Okinawa. You will read two stories about combat from a dear friend of mine, Vern Bluhm. One story is about his days as a tail gunner in a SBD dive-bomber while attached to the USS Saratoga (CV-3). The other is about his stint on Guadalcanal with the Marines.

The Korean War became the Forgotten War. The Vietnam War was the first war that we have fought where protests became a large part of every day life. Any time I wore my uniform in those days, some jeered me. I was spit on by the brother of one of my high school classmates who died in Vietnam. He was a Marine. I always talk trash about our Marines with no offense intended. I always say that the Marines do have their "few good men", Navy corpsmen. Sailors are not always stationed aboard ships. Navy corpsmen, Navy doctors and nurses and chaplains all serve with the Marines. Navy corpsmen and chaplains are known for their bravery under fire. Many are recipients of the Navy's highest award, Congressional Medal of Honor. I have included the citations of those who earned that medal during the Korean and Vietnam wars.

Mark Bell tells about what he did in the Middle East and about his health problems afterwards. I have stories about some of the places I flew to in the Gulf delivering classified keying material and cryptographic equipment and some of the places I stayed during Operation Desert Shield as we developed war time telecommunications plans for aircraft carrier battle groups that would soon be arriving for the upcoming Desert Storm.

A former shipmate, Brian Studnicky, who I did not know (even though we were onboard at the same time) has a story on morals and ethics from the USS Independence (CV-62). As he and I began to communicate, he jarred my brain a little and I began to think of other things that were not so kosher on the Indy. So I have a few stories from the Indy as well as the Belleau Wood.

I am also a professional speaker so I try stories out on my Toastmasters clubs before I give them elsewhere. I was going through my speech archives and came across a few stories that would fit in with morals and ethics as well as patriotic stories with a tribute to a great admiral.

Many people enjoyed my last book on the Navy. I hope that you will enjoy this book as well.

As a final part of this introduction I am including "The Sailor's Creed", the "United States Navy Chief Petty Officer Creed", and the "Code of a Naval Officer" which was written by John Paul Jones in the early years of our country. I feel very deeply about each of the creeds and codes because I served as an enlisted man before becoming an officer. I was dedicated to this country, its history and traditions and to keeping this country free from tyranny and harm from outside forces. The 9/11 incident sparked a renewal of patriotism in this country not seen since World War II. I hope and pray that we never see another time in history where we become complacent and let our guard down.

Have fun reading. You can send any comments to my e-mail at dongoose@aol.com.

The Sailor's Creed
by Author Unknown
Contributed by Donald Johnson

I am a United States Sailor.
I will support and defend
the Constitution of the United States of America,
and I will obey the orders of those appointed over me.
I represent the fighting spirit of the Navy
and those who have gone before me
to defend freedom and democracy around the world.
I proudly serve my country's Navy combat team
with honor, courage and commitment.
I am committed to excellence
and the fair treatment of all.

Chief Petty Officer Creed
by Author Unknown
Contributed by Donald Johnson

During the course of this day you have been caused to humbly accept challenge and face adversity. This you have accomplished with rare good grace. Pointless as some of these challenges may have seemed, there were valid, time-honored reasons behind each pointed barb. It was necessary to meet these hurdles with blind faith in the fellowship of Chief Petty Officers. The goal was to instill in you that trust is inherent with the donning of the uniform of a Chief. It was our intent to impress upon you that challenge is good; a great and necessary reality which cannot mar you—which, in fact, strengthens you. In your future as a Chief Petty Officer., you will be forced to endure adversity far beyond that imposed upon you today. You must face each challenge and adversity with the same dignity and good grace you demonstrated today. By experience, by performance, and by testing, you have been this day advanced to Chief Petty Officer. In the United States Navy—and only in the United States Navy—the rank of E7 carries with it unique responsibilities and privileges you are now bound to observe and expected to fulfill. Your entire way of life is now changed. More will be expected of you; more will be demanded of you. Not because you are a E7 but because you are now a Chief Petty Officer. You have not merely been promoted one pay grade, you have joined an exclusive fellowship and, as in all fellowships, you have a special responsibility to your comrades, even as they have a special responsibility to you. This is why we in the United States Navy may maintain with pride our feelings of accomplishment once we have attained the position of Chief Petty Officer. Your new responsibilities and privileges do not appear in print. They have no official standing; they cannot be referred to by name, number, or file. They have existed for over 100 years, Chiefs before you have freely accepted responsibility beyond the call of printed assignment. Their actions and their performance demanded the respect of their seniors as well as their juniors. It is now required that you be the fountain of wisdom, the ambassador of good will, the authority in personal relations as well as in technical applications. "Ask the Chief" is a household phrase in and out of the Navy. You are now the Chief. The exalted position you have now achieved—and the word exalted is used advisedly—exists because of the attitude and performance of the Chiefs before you. It shall exist only as long as you and your fellow Chiefs maintain these standards. It was our intention that you never forget this day. It was our intention to test you, to try you, and to accept you. Your performance has assured us that you will wear "the hat" with the same pride as your comrades in arms before you. We take a deep and sincere pleasure in clasping your hand, and accepting you as a Chief Petty officer in the United States Navy.

Code of a Naval Officer
By John Paul Jones
Contributed by Donald Johnson

It is, by no means, enough that an officer of the Navy should be a capable mariner. He must be that, of course, but also a great deal more. He should be, as well, a gentleman of liberal education, refined manner, punctilious courtesy, and the nicest sense of personal honor. He would be able to express himself clearly and with force in his own language both with tongue and pen, but he should be versed in French and Spanish.

He should be the soul of tact, patience, justice, firmness, and charity. No meritorious act of a subordinate should escape his attention or be left to pass without its reward, if even the reward be only one single word of approval. Conversely, he should not be blind to a single fault in any subordinate, though at the same time he should be quick and unfailing to distinguish error from malice, thoughtlessness from incompetence, and well-meant shortcoming from heedless or stupid blunder. As he should be universal and impartial in his rewards and approval of merit, so should he be judicial and unbending in his punishment or reproof of misconduct.

Chapter 1

Ports of Call

There are so many ports that Navy ships visit. I had visited many of the places below and would have liked to visit others had I been given a chance to transfer to the east coast.

San Francisco (Fleet Week), Portland, Seattle, Pearl Harbor, Guam, Saipan, Tinian, Yokosuka, Sasebo, Okinawa, Subic Bay, Pusan, Pohang, Kaoshiung, Keelung, Taichung, Hong Kong, DaNang, Cam Ranh Bay, Bangkok, Pattaya Beach, Phuket, Singapore, Perth, Fremantle, Diego Garcia, Mombasa, Bahrain, Aden, Naples, Rota, Athens, Malta, Nice, London, Guantanamo Bay, St. Thomas, Rio de Janiero, Kingston, Panama City, Puerto Vallarta, Mazatlan

Memories of Subic Bay
By Donald Johnson

Joy Club #1, Joy Club #2, New Jolo's Club, Old Jolo's Club, Mom's Club, D'Cave Club, Kong's Restaurant, Ocean's 11, Brown Fox. And the names keep on going.

Many sailors and Marines have special memories of those names and many others. These names were the names of clubs and restaurants in Olongapo City outside of the Subic Bay Naval Base in the Philippines. There were over 300 clubs and restaurants and mini-hotels on or off the main drag, Magsaysay Drive.

The Navy had tried for years to make operational security or OPSEC a top priority among its forces; however, every bar girl (I will refer to the bar girls as Filipinas from here on) in Olongapo knew when the ships were coming into port. There would be signs hung everywhere outside of bars and restaurants with greetings like "Welcome USS Guadalupe" or "Welcome sailors and Marines of USS Peoria".

Visits to Magsaysay Drive in Olongapo were special to many a sailor and Marine. After being out to sea for a few weeks, everyone wanted to go out and party and in the early days change into civilian clothes off the base. In the seventies that changed when civilian clothes were allowed shipboard. I could not tell you how many sets of dress whites I had to buy to replace the red dirt/mud stained uniforms.

Olongapo City was the most fun town in Asia. Many articles have been written about Olongapo and those articles have caused friction between sailors and marines and their spouses because of its nickname of "Sin City". For the new sailors and Marines, it was their chance to experience a celebrated night in Olongapo. For those old salts, it gave them a chance to visit old hangouts and look for their old Filipina friends. For the establishment owners it meant lots of pesos. In the Philippines, Americans had what they called, "Peso-nality", which meant personality with money.

It meant much needed income for the Filipinas and their families and possibly marriage if the right sailor or Marine came in. This was a way of living for them. I know many a sailor who got married their first time in Olongapo.

If you were lucky enough not to get Shore Patrol duty or Quarterdeck watches, you would be in for a lot of fun that first night import. I know I can remember my first night ever in the exciting metropolis of Olongapo City. I was stationed aboard USS Guadalupe (AO-32). I had heard stories from all of the senior petty officers onboard and from a couple of uncles who served in the Pacific at one time or another over the years.

I wasn't new to the ship since I had reported aboard a few months prior to the deployment but was still fairly new to the Navy being a Seaman (E-3) on our first visit to the Philippines.

I was so excited about that first night in Subic. When liberty call was sounded, off we went. We caught the first cab to the Sampaguita Club on base where we got something to eat, something other than shipboard food. San Miguel beer was ten cents and mixed drinks were twenty cents. Slot machines were clinking away in the game room.

A Filipino band, The Fabulous Electros, was playing that night. That band had toured the U.S. with the Beach Boys, Jan and Dean, The Association and other groups in the early 1960's. They played songs by all of those groups and their specialty was the Beach Boys. One of the singers could do a mean imitation of "Purple Haze" by Jimi Hendrix. They were the greatest imitating entertainers that I have ever heard. I would hear many more bands over the years that would be great at imitating American bands, but none as great as The Fabulous Electros.

After some San Miguel beer and a few songs, we decided to head for town. We could hear the music even before we arrived at the gates going into town. If I had been a first time visitor to the base and did not have some of the more experienced sailors with me, I would have found my way to the main gate. I would have followed the deafening roar of the bass guitars emitted by the bands in the clubs near the gate.

After showing our IDs to the Marines at the front gate, we walked over a bridge that crossed the Olongapo River also known as "S—River." That name was very appropriate for the river, since many of the binjo ditches filled with raw sewage were dumped into it. I remember using those binjo ditches many times..

Scantily clad young Filipinas and young boys in little, flimsy boats called "banca boats" signaled from below, asking us sailors and Marines to toss pesos or centavos into the river. I did not have any pesos or centavos that first night, so I threw them a few American coins. They liked American money better, because it was worth more. When I threw the coins, the boys dove into the sewage filled river and somehow came up with the coins and with a smile on their faces.

I would always exchange my dollars for pesos in town because I received a better rate than at the money exchange inside the main gate. Money changers were usually young girls who sat in small glass paned booths. They would try to attract your attention by tapping something on the counters or the glass. Once I filled my wallet, I had peso-nality and was ready to party.

We walked about a half a block down to a club called Oceans Eleven. We had a couple of San Miguel beers and then left for Jolo's Club which later became Old Jolo's. As we were walking down towards Jolo's, I began to feel ill to my stomach. I had drunk about a dozen beers since leaving the ship at 3:30pm. It was now about 7:30pm. We jaywalked on Magsaysay Drive and a jeepney almost hit me. I turned and vomited all over the jeepney. I have always been reminded of that night when I watched "The Flight of the Intruder" where one of the Navy pilots vomited in the back of jeepney after he asked the driver if he had room for a pizza and a six-pack.

We continued on down to Jolo's and joking with all the girls all the way down until we got to our destination. Along the way we heard every type of music imaginable and it all kind of blended together, pop music, country music, heavy metal and folk music.

The smell of street side barbeques with some type of meat on a stick was mixed with the sweet perfume of the Filipinas and the salt air of the Subic Bay and the exhaust of the jeepneys and motorized trikes. There were bright neon lights as far as you could see down Magsaysay Drive. I had the feeling that I was in paradise especially after being at sea for a few weeks. I needed beer, something good to eat and some loving. Being a single young adult male and raised in the 60's during the sexual revolution, I thought I was in heaven. This was almost better than Knott's Berry Farm and Disneyland.

That first night in Jolo's we began to chat with the young Filipinas and bought them drinks so they would continue to sit with us. One of the senior petty officers (PO1) in our radio shack was married to a Filipina. He said something to the young Filipina I was sitting with, and the next thing I know we were in a room upstairs having sex. The PO paid for my first time. I was considered a cherry boy since this was my first time in the PI.

The second night over was a little different. The PO1 that I was running with hooked up with a young Filipina the night before, and she had invited him to the apartment complex where she lived. This is when I really got a good look at how the people of Olongapo lived.

The PO1's girlfriend had a few of her female friends come up for a little party so we could all get to know them. I selected an older woman. By the end of the evening I was in her apartment and I stayed all night. After that night I stayed with her every evening or all day on Saturdays when we were in port.

I, however, strayed from time to time and did end up with an STD. I gave my girlfriend the STD. I paid for her to be treated at the medical clinic in town.

After that deployment overseas, I decided that I would use protection. STDs are not good. I look back now and wished that I had done that from the first time. I have had urinary tract problems a few times since then and I believe that it is because of that first deployment overseas and not using protection and catching the STD.

I developed a soft spot in my heart for the Filipinas because they were doing what they needed to do to support their families. Some of the Filipinas had children and I never wanted to see those children go hungry, so I was always giving the Filipina that I took up with extra money to buy food for her children and family. Many of the Filipinas took care of their parents. I felt that was commendable and honorable.

It is distressing that many of the Filipinas did prostitute themselves in an effort to climb out of poverty; and it is equally distressing that many of us military men in our younger, wilder days did nothing to hinder those situations. I feel that many of us promoted it. And because of that many of the Filipinas who once worked in the bars and clubs of Olongapo have not been accepted and have been dealt with extreme disrespect and unkindness, especially by their own countrymen. The negative taunts usually come from people who have never been in the hopeless state these girls were in. It's easy to call these poor Filipinas "whores", because they traveled to Olongapo or Subic to work in bars and clubs that accommodated sailors and Marines. But I challenge anyone who are familiar with Filipino culture to state that these girls traveled hundreds of miles, from as far as the Cebu, to a place they didn't know, to work in unfamiliar surroundings full of loud music, strangers, and often turmoil, simply because they wanted to mess around.

Don't ask them what they did; ask them why they did it. The fact is that most of these "whores" now have husbands whom they care for, and children whom they are reading to, driving to school, and tucking into bed each night. They have regrets and hopes and souls just as I do now for what I did. They are good people and they are no better and no worse than those who would have them removed from Filipino history. For all of you who have criticized these girls, I can only recommend that you demonstrate compassion, and to let these women go on with their new lives as you go about yours.

I am now an ordained minister and as I look back at all of the sinful things that I did in my younger days I think about what I shoulda, coulda, woulda done. I have asked God for forgiveness and I have repented for all of those past sins.

There is a parable in the Bible that deals with adultery which could apply to any sin, including prostitution, bearing false witness, etc.

In the New Testament in the Gospel According to John 8: 3-11, the scholars and the Pharisees brought to Jesus a woman who had been caught in adultery and they made her stand in front of him. "Teacher," they said to him, "this woman was caught in the act of adultery. In the Law, Moses ordered us to throw stones at such a woman until she was dead. What do you say we should do?"

They asked Jesus this question to test him hoping that his answer would give them something to accuse him of. But Jesus crouched and with his finger wrote in the dust that covered the ground. Still, they kept asking him what should be done, so eventually he stood up and said, "Anyone among you who is without sin, let him throw the first stone." Then he crouched down again, and again began writing in the dust.

Convicted by their own consciences, each man slowly left the oldest and wisest leaving first until not a single accuser remained. Now there was only the woman, and Jesus. When they were alone, Jesus stopped writing and stood up. He looked at her and said, "Woman, where are your accusers? Didn't anyone condemn you?" "No one, my Lord," she said. "Neither do I condemn you," he said. "Now, go forth, and sin no more."

Many of these Filipinas who lived this life of prostitution have moved on in life. I have asked for forgiveness for my sins and I know many of the Filipinas who lived a life of sin have done so, too.

The Copyright Pirate Capital of the World
By Donald Johnson

My first visit to Taiwan was in 1970 after the Guadalupe came off the line in Vietnam. We were going to make a quick two day stop in Kaohsiung for some R&R and then back to Subic Bay to refuel before heading back out to the line to begin refueling operations once again.

I only had one day to do anything in Kaohsiung and guess what I decided to do? You got it. Get a hotel room, get drunk and get laid. I wished I had not done that because I came down with a bad case of gonorrhea. I would learn something from this visit. I thought I was going to be discharged from the Navy for catching this STD. It was my third time on this first time overseas. I learned to use protection from then on out.

My next two visits to Taiwan were in 1976 and 1978 while I was stationed aboard the USS Peoria (LST-1183).

In 1976 we visited Keelung. Keelung was one of those ports that sailors love, lots of booze and available sex with cheap rooms. I decided to hit the bars and drink, get drunk, harass the bar girls and go back to the ship to sleep off the drunk. I had my first experience with community (unisex) restrooms. I don't remember them from my 1970 port call, but this time I was in for a real shocker. I had gone back to use the urinal and as I was standing there doing my thing, a young Chinese woman came in and walked over to a commode and squatted to use the bathroom. There were no doors on the stalls. I could not believe it. But then after thinking about American morals, we are so hung up on things like that. Those countries have a lot less problem with rape, incest and premarital than the Western world.

The next two days a couple of my steaming buddies and I went to Taipei, the capital of Taiwan, for some sightseeing and shopping. I bought mostly clothing on this trip. Taipei was a great city to shop. American women would love to shop there. They would probably have a problem with the unisex restrooms, though.

In 1978 we visited Taichung which was just opened to U.S. Navy ships not too long before that. However, this was going to be the last port of call for any U.S.

Navy ship to Taiwan. President Carter shut that down to appease the Communist Chinese. This was about the same time that Taiwan which had held a permanent veto seat on the United Nations Security Council as Nationalist China was going to lose that seat to the Communists. The U.S. had just recognized Communist China as the rightful owner of that Security Council seat.

Taichung was a great port to visit. The Taiwanese had built the port up to handle all sizes of ships. They had built new hotels and a great shopping area in the downtown area. We had to take a bus from the port to downtown.

This time I decided to buy more than clothes. I had a couple of Volkswagens at home and an AMC Gremlin. I bought the repair manuals for all of those cars. I also bought more clothing for myself, Barbara and the girls. I then decided to buy several LP records and (get this!) eight-track tapes. I bought some Beatles, Beach Boys, Jan and Dean, Oldies but Goodies, Kenny Rogers and Dolly Parton.

The repair manuals were great to have. You could tell that they were copies and not the real thing. I was told after we got back to the states that I had broken a law by bringing them back into the states. At that time I did not care. These manuals cost me about $5.00 a piece. Those manuals would have cost me $50.00 a piece in the states. When I got home, I fixed every problem that I had with the cars. Instead of having a repair shop do the work, I did all of it myself.

As for the LP records and 8-track tapes, they were great copies of the real thing. I bought pirated music at $1.00 per record and tape. These records and tapes were just as good as the ones I would have bought in the states at $12.95. I have since put those records on CDs and sold the records on eBay.

Do I regret buying them? Back then I didn't. Today? Yes, because I am recording all of my sermons on CD and selling them. I would not want anyone pirating my copyrighted CDs.

Golf and Mar John
By Donald Johnson

We had just left Hong Kong and were headed for Singapore. I had reported to the USS Belleau Wood (LHA-3) the day before we pulled into Hong Kong. I left San Diego after getting my family settled in our new home. We had just come down from Adak, Alaska. I was so glad to get back to sea after that bad duty station. I knew I was going to get passed over for Lieutenant the first time around because of the two bad fitness reports that the CO up there had given me.

My trip to catch the ship took me in a round about way. I had to fly from San Diego to Los Angeles to catch a charter flight, Trans-America Airlines. That flight took me to McChord AFB, WA, Elmendorf AFB, AK, Kadena AB, Okinawa and finally to the Clark AB, Philippines. That flight must have taken 24 hours. I don't like flying anyway so I was totally tired when we got to Clark Air Base near Angeles City, The Philippines. There were no rooms at the BOQ so I had to get me a hotel room in town. I took a cab out into town and decided on a nice looking hotel based on the recommendation of the driver. He was totally right. It was a good hotel. I got me a room, took a quick shower and put some clean clothes on. I then headed downstairs for a good meal and a San Miguel beer. It only took three beers to tell me that I needed a good sleep. I went back up to my room and fell asleep until 6am. I caught a cab back to the base to catch a bus to Subic Bay Naval Station.

When I got to Subic, I checked in with the BOQ and base personnel. The personnel office told me that the ship would be pulling into port in eight weeks. I did not want to wait for the ship that long. Being a Navy communicator, I went over to the local Naval Telecommunications Center and talked with the Officer In Charge. He allowed for me to send a message to the ship and have them make arrangements for my earlier transfer.

In a couple of days I get an answer back telling me that they would set up an earlier transfer date than eight weeks because the current Radio Officer wanted to leave. Ten days later I was on a Navy flight to Okinawa to catch the USS Dubuque that would take me to within a few hundred yards of the Belleau Wood that would then send a helo over to pick me and others up for transfer.

A day out of Hong Kong I got my first helicopter ride. To tell you the truth, I like riding in helicopters better than planes.

My stay in Hong Kong this time was uneventful. I went over one day for a good meal and some Hong Kong beer. I was trying to complete the turnover with the Radio Officer so we could get him out of there soon. He really did not leave until about a month later when we got to Australia.

I began to get acquainted with all of the senior petty officers from the PO1s to the Chiefs. The leading chief petty officer was RMC Treece who had served with me in Hawaii when we were both RM1s together. Chief Treece had changed considerably and was actually getting ready to make Senior Chief (E-8). One of the RM1s, Jim Kelly, was upset that he had not made chief yet, so I wanted to get to know him better so that I could see what made him tick and then I could write a performance evaluation that would have the wording that would make the selection board take note. So I told Jim that we would go out and do something together when we got to Singapore. He was a golfer and I had not golfed since leaving Hawaii. So we decided on a round of golf and a night out on the town.

I made reservations for Jim and I for the golf course via the Special Services officer onboard who sent a Naval message to the Naval Office in Singapore. When the Belleau Wood arrived in Singapore, she had to moor out in the harbor and we had to take a water taxi in. Once we got ashore we took a cab out to the golf course.

Jim and I got our rented golf clubs. We were told that we had to have golf caddies, not the kind with wheels. They assigned two guys to us for the 18 holes. Now we were ready for some golf.

I was so rusty. I double and triple bogeyed the first four holes. Jim was doing a little better than me. At about the 10th hole, my caddy walked up to me and told me to change my stance a little. He showed me how to place my legs and feet. That helped quite a bit. I bogeyed the next couple of holes. When we got to the 16th hole, it began raining. I mean raining, heavy. We got under a hutch at that hole because a lightning storm was beginning to take affect. I wasn't about to become a statistic to lightning storms.

The storm appeared that it was not going to stop any time too soon. We decided to wait another 15-30 minutes to see if it cleared. During that time we tried to strike up a conversation with the caddies. My caddy spoke very little English. He spoke just enough. I had lit up a cigarette and asked him if he wanted an American cigarette. He took one from me. Then he began asking us if we wanted some mar john. I thought he was asking for my pack of Marlboro cigarettes. I had only brought enough with me to get through the day and did not want to give him my unopened pack. That is not what he was trying to say. He kept asking us if we wanted some of his mar john. I didn't know what he was saying and neither did Jim.

I finally said, "Yes." What did he do next? He took his cigarette pack out of his shirt pocket and produced a marijuana cigarette. When he did that, then I knew what he was trying to say.

Wow! I did not want any of that. This caddie then lit it up and tried to get me to smoke some. I told him, "No, I don't like mar john." Jim did the same. My caddy let his buddy have a couple of tokes. He kept trying to get Jim and me to take a couple of tokes. We kept turning him down.

We decided then to grab our clubs and head back to the club house and turn our clubs in and leave. We did not want to be around the mar john smoking caddies. We knew that drug use in Singapore was a bad offense and in some cases was punishable by death. I know that I was not ready for that, so I decided to get us out of that situation.

Once we were back at the club house, we turned our clubs in and asked for them to call a cab for us. The cab was there in about 15 minutes. I was so glad to get out of there.

Jim and I went to the American Club for dinner and met up with some other guys from the Radio Shack and then headed out for a night of drinking on Boogey Street. That is where all of the transvestites come out. A bunch of us sat at a table and made fun of them all night long. We finally caught a cab back to fleet landing about midnight or so.

I will never forget that golf game and Mar John.

Thai Seafood Pizza
By Donald Johnson

I had only been on the Belleau Wood for less than a month and we were hitting all the ports that I wanted to see again or see for the first time. I had always wanted to go back to Pattaya Beach, Thailand. I had been there in 1976 on the USS Peoria (LST-1183) and loved it. I had purchased my wife a nice black star sapphire ring. She still has it today.

This time (1984) the ship was not going to Pattaya Beach. It was going to anchor off Phuket Island on the western side of the Thai peninsula. It was a resort island that many Europeans visited. It was part of what was called the Thai Riviera. That place brought back memories to me when I saw that the tsunami of December of 2004 had hit the resort island. This visit was 20 years before.

The Belleau Wood had anchored off the western side of the island near Patong Beach where that tsunami hit. I went over on the first boat. So did my Signals Officer, a young ensign by the name of Andy. I don't recall his last name. We got a room together at one of the beach hotels that had bungalows.

Patong Beach had beaches that were clothing optional. The beach hotel that Andy and I got had one of those beaches. So I got an eye full. As I was sitting on the beach I noticed the seas beginning to pick up. The ship was having a problem at anchor. The shore patrol (SP) officer came up to me and told me that the ship needed me back on board to help move the ship around to the other side of the island and anchor off the harbor to the city Phuket.

Before I left to catch a boat back to the ship, I noticed a young Marine harassing a woman who was lying on a lounge chair in the nude. She was trying to tell him to leave her alone. I believe she was German because she kept telling him, Nein. I remember a little German and that to me met, No.

I decided to go rescue her. I identified myself to the Marine. He was drunk already. He gave me a ration of "you know what". I then yelled out for the SP officer who was nearby. I told the SP officer what was going on. He and two of his SP took the Marine into custody and were going to escort him back to the ship with us. The German woman said, Danke, which means Thank you.

I got back to the ship and helped with moving the ship around to the other side of the island. I then left on the first boat to Phuket. I hooked up with one of my chiefs and a few of my radiomen. It was some what late in the evening. We went and got something to eat and then hit a bar.

As we were sitting there drinking with the music blasting away, a few girls came over and sat down with us. One of them sat next to me. I was in no mood to take a prostitute back to my bungalow. I just wanted to relax on the beach in Patong. I did decide to dance with this girl. She wasn't too bad looking in the dim light. As we were dancing on the floor, she grabbed my crotch and tried to get me all worked up. I thought to myself that I could do that, too. I grabbed her between her legs and Lo and Behold! I grabbed more than I was expecting. I immediately let go and back away. I told her/him that I was not going to sit with her/him any longer.

As soon as I separated from her/him, one of my radiomen in another group sitting across the dance floor from me and my group went up to her/him and asked her/him to dance. I then thought it was kind of humorous. I sat there for about another 30 minutes and watched everyone. Before too long, that young radioman was feeling her/him up and kissing her/him. I nearly vomited knowing who this person was.

I left the club and grabbed a cab to take me to the other side of the island to my bungalow. When I got there, Andy was sleeping and sawing some big logs. I grabbed a beer out of the refrigerator and turned the TV on and watched a movie for a while. I fell asleep soon thereafter. I guess Andy woke up in the middle of the night and shut the TV off.

In the morning, Andy and I went out walked around town and just window shopped and talked to the shop owners and sidewalk café and restaurant owners. All we did for the next three days was to just relax on the beach and sat in the sidewalk cafés and ate everything from Thai food to pizza. They had a seafood pizza I thought was out of this world. I ate one each day. They put shrimp, octopus, shark, and other types of fish on the pizza. I am a seafood addict. I love seafood. I gorged myself.

Andy and I left on the fourth day to go back to the ship for the night and would be up early the next morning to help get the ship underway. I believe Andy was the junior Officer of the Deck (JOOD) for getting underway.

I woke up in the morning with a rumbling stomach. I felt nauseous. I went to the head to take care of my rumbling stomach. I went to breakfast and within an hour or so after eating I had to rush to the head.

For the next seven days on our way to Australia, I spent many hours sitting on the commode. I went to sick call each day. The doc did not want to give me anything to stop the flow. He thinks what caused my problem was not fully cooked or raw seafood. There were a few others on board with the same problem. They had eaten at the same establishments that I had. I did eat some raw oysters.

On the sixth day of our voyage to Australia, I told the doc to give me some Kaopectate to clog me up. He did not want to, because he wanted me to flush my system with lots of liquid. I told him that I had been drinking over two gallons of water a day and it wasn't doing anything. He finally relented and gave me a bottle of Kaopectate. It took about four hours but finally the flow stopped. The stomach cramps went away and my bottom began to heal.

I learned two things. The first thing I learned was that the young radioman who took my girl/transvestite back to a hotel room and found out very quickly that she was not a girl. He kicked the transvestite out of his room.

When I saw him onboard the ship after getting underway for Australia, I asked him if he had fun with that nice looking woman. I had a big smile on my face. He was really mad. He said you knew that she was not a she, didn't you? I told him that I did, but thought I would let things go. I told him that I knew he would eventually find out that she was a transvestite.

The second thing I learned was that I should not eat uncooked food in any of the third world countries. I have never experience stomach problems like that since. I do not wish that kind of problem on anyone.

As for the port visit, I really enjoyed myself and it was a nice relaxing port.

Swan River Wine Cruise
by Donald Johnson

The Belleau Wood was pulling into Fremantle, Australia after being at sea for seven days. We had left Phuket Island, Thailand. I was finally well from seven days of Montezuma's Revenge. We were to be in port for only two days before pulling out and spending a week or ten days doing military operations with the Australian Navy, Marines and Army.

When we pulled back into port after the operations, we had a scheduled reception at the Fremantle Yacht Club for all of the ship's officers, Navy and Marines. There were about 200 of us. The Yacht Club invited over 300 women. That Yacht Club was so packed that you could barely turn around. The two junior officers that worked for me and I left with three women and went into Perth to a couple of night clubs to go dancing. I caught a cab back to the ship after a night of drinking and dancing. I had the duty the next day.

After getting up the next morning, I checked in with the duty section leader to find out what watch I had. I had the 1200-1600 OOD watch on the quarterdeck. The ship had already experience a nuclear protest on the flight deck. Somehow the protestors acted like tourists and when they got to the flight deck, they decided to pull their banners out and start their protest. We had to get the Fremantle Police to help get them off our ship. We did not feel like having a big media presence during this port visit.

I had some time on my hands, so I went down to Special Services to see what types of tours they had and saw that they had a Wine Cruise scheduled for the next day and that there were a few seats left. I signed up. The rest of the day was uneventful.

On the third day in port, I awoke and got ready for the Wine Cruise. This cruise was to take us up the Swan River from Perth to their "Napa Wine Country" to Houghton Vineyards.

We boarded a bus on the pier that would take us to the location in Perth to board the wine cruise boat. The boat reminded me of the Jungle Cruise boats at Disneyland with wooden benches that sat three people on both sides of the boat. They had a section in the back for restrooms and a bar.

I hooked up with one of the civilian college instructors that were traveling with us. We had a few PACE courses ongoing. I don't remember his name, but I know that he was a good guy and he did drink. There were many Belleau Wood sailors and Marines on the boat. About two dozen or so civilians were on the boat as well. Many were Eastern Australians out from the Sydney area vacationing, somewhat like New Yorkers coming to the San Francisco Bay area to vacation.

At 8:30am they start serving us champagne coolers. Many of us sailors had not eaten anything yet, so we were drinking on empty stomachs. I had about four champagne coolers before we reached our destination at about 10:30am. When we reached our destination which was several miles from Houghton Vineyards, we had to wait for buses to come pick us up which was about a 15 minute wait.

The buses took us to Houghton Vineyards. The winery had set up several tasting tables with about 12-15 bottles of different types of wine on each table. Each table had the exact same bottles on them. I stood at one of the tables and I must have sampled every bottle at least twice and the white burgundy three times. I fell in love with the white burgundy.

At about 11:30am, they began the tour of the winery and it took about 45 minutes. That gave me some time to let the champagne and wine to settle before our scheduled lunch. I sure am glad the lunch was included. I was hungry and somewhat drunk. When the tour was over, they took us into the large dining facility and sat us down. The instructor and I were sitting across from a couple from Sydney and we talked for a long time. They had seen the TV the day before and the protest that happened on our ship. They were disgusted at the protestors. There were eight of us sitting at that table and six bottles of wine. There were four different types of white wine and two types of red wine. I had a bottle of red burgundy in front of me and I was not overly fond of it. The Australian woman had a bottle of white burgundy in front of her and wanted to trade. So I did. Now I had a bottle of white burgundy to share with my drinking partner. We popped the corks and began pouring. I was so drunk that when they brought the food in, I just ate. To this day, I don't remember what they served.

After lunch we got up and started for the buses. I found a full bottle of white burgundy on one of the tables and I stopped to pick it up and took it with me. The bottle had been opened but the cork put back in. I popped the cork once we were one the bus and began drinking from the bottle. I passed it around as we rode the bus down to the landing.

We boarded the boat at about 2pm. We would arrive back in Perth at about 4pm. I was getting drunker and drunker, but I remembered everything that was going on around me. There were three Belleau Wood sailors sitting in front of me and my drinking partner. They were bothering three young women and would not leave them alone. I was getting a little hot under the collar. I told them to leave them alone. They wanted to know who I was. I told them I knew they were from the Belleau Wood and so was I and if they did not know who I was, they would find out when we got back to the ship. They would be up in front of the XO in no time. They decided not to test me. One of the sailors sitting next to the guard rail was really drunk (drunker than me) and leaned over and began vomiting into the river. He finally passed out.

I recharged my glass with champagne coolers all the way back. I must have had about four more. When we arrived at the landing in Perth, I was so drunk that I could barely walk. I had a hard time lifting my feet up the steps to get off and then when we got out to the street, I had a hard time lifting my feet up over the six inch curb. My drinking partner and I walked down to where we could catch a cab to take us back to the ship.

When we got back, I had a hard time walking up the gangway, but finally made it and made it down to my stateroom. I slept from about 5:30pm until 6:00am the next morning.

On the first night in, I had set up a dinner date with the woman I had gone out dancing with. The dinner date was set up for the day after the Wine Cruise. I didn't much feel like going out, but she wanted to buy me dinner. I was going to let her. When she picked me up for dinner, she told me that the reason for the dinner was to interview me for her magazine. She was the managing editor for the Western Australia magazine. When we got to the restaurant, we ordered our meal and then she began her interviewing process. She asked about my career in the Navy and about my family and about my plans after retirement. I remember her being a beautiful woman, a single mother with a 16 year old son. She took me by her home to meet her son and then took me back to the ship.

I will never forget that time in Australia mainly for the Wine Cruise, but I will always remember that woman because of the interview and dinner. I had never experienced a situation where a woman would buy me dinner. That was a first.

A Japanese Tour
by Donald Johnson

In late 1970 we had just come off the line in Vietnam and headed to Yokosuka, Japan. This would be our only stop in this port. I was ready for beer and women. I was in for a big surprise when it came to women.

The enlisted club was located outside the base a couple of blocks to right of the gate on the left hand side. It was a three story building with a couple of eating places, E1-E4 had their club, E5-E6 had their Acey Deucy Club and the Chiefs Club was on the third floor. There was also a wine and liquor store and a small shopping area within this building. The Haunch were all the bars and girls were located was within a block of the enlisted club.

We went to the Haunch looking for women and we found out that all they wanted was for us to buy them drinks. Prostitution was outlawed in Japan and it would be harder to find women to have sex with. We all just got drunk that night and headed back to the ship. The next day I had the duty but I did sign up for a tour the day after along with a few of the other radiomen.

The day of the tour came and we went down to the pier to catch the bus for the tour. At this time of my career the Navy had still not allow sailors E6 and below to have civilian clothes on board. We all wore our dress blues with our Navy blue watch sweater under our jumper to keep us warm that day. It was becoming winter in Japan and the morning chill was the only clue we needed.

The tour was going to take us to some Buddha temples, take us on a mountain lake cruise on a glass bottom boat, then to lunch. After lunch it would be into the mountains and a tram ride up the side of a mountain into the sulfur springs and then back to town to end the tour.

The first stop was to the Buddha temples. I had a cheap 110 camera and took a few pictures. I am a history buff so I read everything that they had out about the temples. The stop was about 30 minutes long.

The second stop was to the mountain lake where we embarked a glass-bottom boat on a crystal clear mountain lake. The scenery was out of an art gallery. The pine trees were a beautiful green and you could smell the pine. The fish below the boat were luminescent. All looked like variable colored neon lights shaped like fish. The boat trip across the lake was very relaxing.

When we got to the other side of the lake, the boat tied up right next to the restaurant that we were going to eat lunch. I had never had Japanese food before so this was going to be a treat. I ordered Sukiyaki as my main dish which was a noodle soup with seafood and meatballs and veggies. They did not tell me that it was very spicy and hot. It was a great lunch. I tried using chopsticks, but decided to use a fork instead. I also had my first taste of sake, a rice wine. It is served lukewarm or at room temperature. I did not care for it.

We then boarded the bus that traveled around the lake to pick us up at the restaurant. It was now to the sulfur springs which were located at the top of a mountain. The bus dropped us at the bottom of the mountain where they had trams to take us to the top. This was another first for me. When you are raised in flatland Kansas, the only thing you see that is unusual is a tornado. I had only been out of state once after my parents resettled in Kansas after my dad was discharged from the Army. He drove us down to Oklahoma for a day when I was about 12 or 13.

We all got into the tram and the cable started pulling us up the side of the mountain. There were four of us radiomen, a yeoman and an engineman in the tram. The engineman was trying to make things exciting as we got to about 300-400 feet above the ground. He decided to start swaying the tram back and forth. We were all afraid that he was going to make it sway too far to one side and cause the tram and us to fall to the mountainside. We all finally had to jump on him and hold him down until we got to the top. I had never felt so scared in my life. When we got off at the top, we headed straight to the bus. The sulfur smell was very strong. The smell of rotten eggs did nothing for me.

On the way back to the ship, the bus stopped at a roadside shopping area so that we could shop and buy something to drink. The only thing that they had in alcoholic beverages was a rot gut whiskey called Nikko and warm Asahi beer. We each bought a pint of Nikko and a pint of Asahi. The rest of the way back we were drinking Nikko and chasing it with Asahi. We were all pretty lit up by the time we got back.

The bus dropped us off and we radiomen decided to go bar hopping in the Haunch. We got out there and went into a bar called the Brass Rails. It was called that because it had brass rails around the dance floor and separating various parts of the club. We had a couple of cold Asahi beers and then decided to try some Akadama wine which is a plum wine and very sweet. The wine came in all sizes of bottles. We bought one that was about a 3 or 4 liter bottle, a huge bottle. We took that bottle with us from bar to bar. At one bar we went into, the crowd was getting really raucous. It was loud and a few sailors were arguing. One of my buddies yelled at someone and that started a fight. The shore patrol came in and began rounding everyone up. We were taken back to the ship and delivered to the quarterdeck. The OOD gave us our IDs back and told us to go down and hit our racks. We did do that. I slept in the next day. I found out that they had a small riot in the Haunch the night before. I guess it started in the last bar we were in and spread to other bars.

There were only two ships in port, the USS Chicago, a large cruiser and us, USS Guadalupe (AO-32). We were scheduled to leave port the next day. It is a good thing, because I saw a message that had asked the Chicago to leave port and not come back for the rest of their deployment. I had a radioman buddy on the Chicago. We had gone to radioman school together. I talked to him in Subic which was our last stop before heading home.

I spent more time in Yokosuka in 1976 when the USS Peoria lost its bow ramp. That is another story later in this book. A quick stopover was made in 1978 on the Peoria and again in 1984 onboard Belleau Wood. I had a story about that port visit in my first book. Then on the way back from Desert Shield the Independence made a three day visit to check out the base since that was going to be the ship's new home port the following year.

In 1991 when the Indy changed home port to Yokosuka from San Diego, I became familiar with Japan all over again. I was going to be there for five months before I came home to retire. This time I felt like hanging out at the officer's club on base and sing karaoke. I had a lot of fun doing that. I did take one tour, but spent a lot of my time watching the ship's basketball team and tackle football team play in the base's league. I was just anxious to retire.

Thank God For COD
By Les Bates

I was the Sales (S-3 Division) Officer on the USS Ranger (CV-61), responsible for the operation of three Ship's Retail Outlets, two soda and snack shops, the laundry and dry cleaning plants, and three barber shops. I was also assigned miscellaneous other collateral duties. The Ranger was the tenth ship that I served on, my first as an officer, and by far the largest. All of my prior service was as a Disbursing Clerk; so the Sales Division was relatively new to me, and an aircraft carrier was a heck of a place to learn the trade. Anywhere else would be a cinch after that.

We commenced our Western Pacific Cruise in February 1979. This was the Ranger's 14th cruise, and it was my tenth Westpac in addition to one Med Cruise, and one South American Cruise. This was one eventful cruise, and I am glad I never had another one like it. But I'll go into that in another story.

About halfway through the cruise, we were scheduled to go to Hong Kong for a 4-day R & R. We were sitting in Subic Bay, completing a short upkeep period. I was working at my desk when one of the Ship's Store Operators walked in and said, "Mr. Bates, I just ordered (from our storeroom) film, and they are out of it." He rattled off 3 or 4 of our best selling films, and said, "We're going to Hong Kong, and everyone is going to want these. There will be some pissed off sailors." The one responsible for re-ordering our merchandise really dropped the ball. I spent the next couple of hours thinking about the situation (What am I going to tell my boss? What about the film needs of 5000 sailors? Where can I get some film? etc. etc.) There was a good size Navy Exchange in Subic Bay, but they would never be able to transfer to us the quantities that we would need, even if they had it.

Somebody above, way above, was really looking out for me that day. I received a phone call from the Quarterdeck that a salesman wanted to see me if possible. To make a long story sort, it was the Kodak Regional Representative. He had just been to the Base Exchange and happened to see this aircraft carrier (us) sitting there, so he just figured that he would pay us a courtesy call to see if we needed anything. I explained the situation to him. He said that he would do his best. I placed an order for close to $50,000 worth of assorted film.

The next day we left Subic and made a leisurely cruise in the general direction of Hong Kong. I say general direction, because we conducted training exercises on the way, and edged over toward Okinawa so we could have regular COD (Carrier Onboard Delivery) flights for the next 2 or 3 days. We took 4 days to get to Hong Kong, when we could make the trip in a day or two very easily. The third day out, we received a partial shipment of our Kodak film. The fourth day, we received another partial shipment of film. Then we arrived in Hong Kong, the rest of the film order came in. Talk about RELIEF!!!

No one outside of me and a couple of Ship's Servicemen ever knew about the "film crisis." My boss had a very biting tongue, and I am glad I didn't have to hear it that day.

Chapter 2

Navy Humor

If you like humor, you will find it here. I wrote the first humorous story. The other stories are penned anonymously. Enjoy and laugh until your heart is content.

"Well," snarled the tough old Chief to the bewildered Seaman. "I suppose after you get discharged, you'll just be waiting for me to die so you can come and pee on my grave."

"Not me, Chief," the Seaman replied. "Once I get out, I'm never going to stand in line again."

—Author Unknown

The Secrets of Leadership
By Donald Johnson

The USS Independence (CV-62) Aircraft Carrier Battle Group was preparing for a weapons exercise in the Indian Ocean when it was called north to provide a combat air patrol over northern Saudi Arabia to keep Saddam from coming across from Kuwait that he had just invaded. We had the Commander of Carrier Group One, commanded by Rear Admiral Lower Half Jerry Unruh. Admiral Unruh made two star on our way to the Gulf, and by the time, we got back to San Diego he received his third star and became Commander, Third Fleet, a fleet command that had not seen sea duty for many, many years. He made it a sea going command again. Admiral Unruh's command was responsible for developing all of the war time plans for all Aircraft Carrier Battle Groups that would participate in Operation Desert Shield. I attended many of his staff meetings because I worked closely with his communications experts. He and I had something in common. We both came from Kansas.

As we were putting our plans together, General Norman Schwarzkopf was putting his plans together in Tampa and then eventually Riyadh, Saudi Arabia. He would visit many of the ships in the Gulf before combat operations began.

He visited the Indy on day and would be a guest of the Admiral's. We were going to put on an air show for him and they wanted him to have a bird's eye view so they decided on an old gun sponson off the signal bridge, but they wanted to make a stand to put inside the gun sponson for him stand on during the air show. The carpenter shop had to make one to hold this big over six foot tall 250 pound man. I tested the stand out before he came up. I figured if it would hold me, it would hold him. When he came up, I chatted with him for just a short period of time before I took him out to the gun sponson. I made sure that it was going to hold him before I left. It did.

I have seen many jokes or humorous stories about military leadership. I came across a humorous anecdote many years ago that I changed to reflect my thoughts on military leadership and would use it when speaking before an audience that was primarily military. I have included Admiral Unruh and General Schwarzkopf in this story that goes like this.

General Schwarzkopf planned a visit to the Indy one day. Admiral Unruh wanted to show the General what he knew about seamanship, so he decided to take the Admiral's barge out for an afternoon of fishing. The barge was a modified motor whale boat with a cabin top and more comfortable seats onboard. There were other necessities inside, too. Admiral Unruh decided that he could be his own coxswain for the afternoon with just him and the General onboard.

When the General arrived, he got the five and dime tour of the ship as the deck department lowered the Admiral's barge into the water and then brought it over to the area where the inport gangway was located and lowered the gangway for the Admiral and General.

When it came time for them to depart on their afternoon fishing expedition, then went down the gangway to board the barge. The Admiral showed his good seamanship skills by pulling the barge away from the ship and headed out.

They found a good fishing place about two miles away from the ship. They were chatting and having a good time fishing when all of sudden one of those Persian Gulf storms began brewing and it came up so quick that the Admiral did not have time to get the barge started to head back to the ship.

The wind began blowing and the waves became white caps. The barge was being tossed around like a rag doll. The barge was then upended tossing the Admiral and the General into the water. The storm stopped as quickly as it began.

The General was handling the situation very well and began swimming back to the upturned barge. As he began swimming he saw the Admiral struggling and decided to go assist him. The Admiral was beginning to go under for the third time when the General reached him.

The General grabbed the Admiral and began swimming and pulling the Admiral with him. It took a little while for them to get there. When they arrived at the barge, the General pushed the Admiral on top of the upturned barge and then climbed up himself.

After both of them were able to catch their breath, the Admiral spoke up. He said, "Norm, can you keep a secret?" Norm told him he could. The Admiral went on, "Norm, don't let the guys know that I can't swim." The General said, "Jerry, your secret is safe with me. Don't tell the guys that I can't walk on water."

Which Service is the Best
By Author Unknown
Contributed by Donald Johnson

A Soldier, Sailor, Airman and Marine got into an argument as to which service was "the best." The arguing became so intense the four servicemen failed to see an oncoming truck. They were struck and killed instantly.

Soon the servicemen found themselves at the Pearly Gates where they met St. Peter. They decided only he could be the ultimate source of truth and honesty. So, the four asked him, "St. Peter, which branch of the United States Armed Forces is the best?" After a few moments he replied that he could not answer that and would have to kick it up to God for an answer the next time he saw Him. Meanwhile, thank you for your service on earth and welcome to Heaven.

Some time later the four see St. Peter and remind him of the question they had asked when first entering Heaven. Suddenly a sparkling white dove lands on St. Peter's shoulder. there is a note, glistening with gold dust, in the dove's beak. "This must be the answer from the Boss, let's see what it says." He opens the note, trumpets blare, gold dust drifts into the air, harps play crescendos, and St. Peter reads aloud to the servicemen.

MEMORANDUM: FROM THE DESK OF THE ALMIGHTY.
TO: Soldiers, Sailors, Airmen and Marines.
SUBJ: WHICH MILITARY SERVICE IS BEST.

Gentlemen, all branches of the United States Armed Forces are honorable and noble. Each serves America well and with distinction. Being servicemen in the United States Military represents a special calling warranting special respect, tribute and dedication. Be proud of that.

Sincerely,
GOD, USN (Ret.)

SAILORISMS
By Author Unknown
Contributed by Donald Johnson

Me and Willy were lollygagging by the scuttlebutt after being aloft to boy-butter up the antennas and were just perched on a bollard eyeballing a couple of bilge rats and flangeheads using crescent hammers to pack monkey shit around a fitting on a handybilly.

All of a sudden the dicksmith started hard-assing one of the deck apes for lifting his pogey bait. The pecker-checker was a sewer pipe sailor and the deck ape was a gator. Maybe being blackshoes on a bird farm surrounded by a gaggle of cans didn't set right with either of those gobs.

The deck ape ran through the nearest hatch and dogged it tight because he knew the penis machinist was going to lie below, catch him between decks and punch him in the snot locker. He'd probably wind up on the binnacle list but Doc would find a way to gundeck the paper or give it the deep six to keep himself above board.

We heard the skivvy waver announce over the bitch box that the bread burners had creamed foreskins on toast and SOS ready on the mess decks so we cut and run to avoid the clusterfuck when the twidgets and cannon cockers knew chow was on.

We were balls to the wall for the barn and everyone was preparing to hit the beach as soon as we doubled-up and threw the brow over. I had a ditty bag full of fufu juice that I was gonna spread on thick for the bar hogs with those sweet Bosnias. Sure beats the hell out of brown bagging. Might even hit the acey duecy club and try to hook up with a Westpac widow. They were always leaving snail trails on the dance floor on amateur night.

If you understand this, you're true blue and gold!

Admiral Rickover's Transfer
By Author Unknown
Contributed by Donald Johnson

At one point in time during his career, Admiral Hyman Rickover, the father of the Nuclear Navy, was commander of a carrier task force, and had his flag on the carrier.

For exercise, Adm. Rickover walked a lap around the flight deck every day. It became custom for the sailors to approach the Admiral during his walks, and gripe, complain, etc., and the Admiral would take care of the problems brought forth by the crew. It was a great morale booster.

Well, the day came when Admiral Rickover was reassigned to Washington, and a helicopter carried him off. The crew was so despondent at his departure that the helmsman wasn't paying attention to his job, and the carrier hit a sandbar.

Yes, they grounded the warship he walked on.

A Dog Named Chief
By Author Unknown
Contributed by Donald Johnson

In the Blue Ridge Mountains, there was a retired sailor who was reputed to have the best hunting dog ever, by the name of "Chief".

Three Admirals went-up into the mountains and wanted to rent him. The old sailor said good hunting dog…gonna cost ya $50.00 a day." They agreed and three days later came back with the limit.

The next year they came back. "Chief" got better, gonna cost you $75.00 a day," again they agreed, and 2 days later they came back with the limit.

The third year they came back and told the old sailor they had to have "Chief" even if it cost $100.00 a day. The old sailor replied, "You can have the worthless mutt for $5.00 a day, and I'm overcharging you $4.00!!"

The bewildered Admirals asked, "But we don't understand, what happened to him?"

"Well, a crew from the Navy base in Norfolk came up and rented him. One of the idiots called him Master Chief, and he's just been sitting on his butt barkin' like heck ever since…"

A Sailor's Promise
By Author Unknown
Contributed by Donald Johnson

I, Don Johnson, in lieu of going to prison, swear to sign 4 years of my life to the US NAVY, because I want to hang out with Marines without actually having to BE one of them, because I thought the Air Force was "too corporate," and because I thought, "Hey, I like to swim…why not?"

I promise to wear clothing that went out of style in 1976 and to have my name stenciled into the butt of every pair of pants I own. I understand that I will be mistaken for the good humor man in the summer and for Waffen SS during the winter.

I will strive to use a different language than the rest of the English speaking world using words like "deck, bulkhead, cover and head" instead of "floor, wall, hat, and toilet." I will take great pride in the fact that all Navy acronyms, rank, and insignia, and everything else for that matter are completely different from the other services and make absolutely no sense whatsoever.

I will muster (whatever that is) at 0700 hrs every morning unless I am buddy-buddy with the chief, in which case I will show up around 0930 hours.

I vow to hone my coffee cup handling skills to the point that I can stand up in a kayak being tossed around in a typhoon and still not spill a DROP. (This applies to beer, also.)

I consent to being promoted and subsequently busted at least twice per fiscal year. I realize that, once selected for chief, I am required to submit myself to sick, and quite possibly illegal, whims of my new-found "colleagues."—so help me Neptune.

Sailor and Marine
By Author Unknown
Contributed by Donald Johnson

A salty Navy Chief and a crusty Marine Gunny Sergeant are at a bar arguing about who had the tougher career.

"I did 30 years in the Recon," the Marine declared proudly, "and fought in three of my country's wars. Fresh out of boot camp, I hit the beach at Okinawa, clawed my way up the blood-soaked sand, and eventually took out an entire enemy machine gun nest with a single grenade."

"As a sergeant, I fought in Korea alongside General MacArthur. We pushed back the enemy inch by bloody inch all the way up to the Chinese border, always under a barrage of artillery and small arms fire."

"Finally, as a gunny sergeant, I did three consecutive combat tours in Vietnam. We humped through the mud and razor grass for 14 hours a day, plagued by rain and mosquitoes, ducking under sniper fire all day and mortar fire at night. In a fire fight, we'd shoot until our arms ached and our guns were empty, then we'd charge the enemy with bayonets!"

Looking straight ahead, the Chief says nothing.

Then after a deliberately long, slow drink, the Chief says, "Yeah, it figures…all shore duty."

Almost Perfect
By Author Unknown
Contributed by Donald Johnson

It seems that a young man volunteered for Navy service during World War II. He had such a high aptitude for aviation that he was sent right to Pensacola skipping boot camp.

The very first day at Pensacola he solos and is the best flier on the base. All they could do was to give him his gold wings and assign him immediately to an aircraft carrier in the Pacific.

On his first day aboard he took off and single-handedly shot down 6 Japanese Zeroes. Then climbing up to 20,000 ft. he found 9 more Japanese planes and shot them all down, too. Noting that his fuel was getting low, he descended, circled the carrier and came in for a perfect landing on the deck.

He threw back the canopy, climbed out and jogged over to the captain. Saluting smartly he said, "Well sir, how did I do on my very first day?"

The captain turned around, bowed, and replied, "You make one velly impoltant mistake!"

WARNING to the Family and Friends of a Returning Sailor
By Author Unknown
Contributed by Donald Johnson

You will soon have your loved one home again. He has been living in an extremely crude environment for quite some time and will require time to adjust to his former lifestyle.

The key to help him through this difficulty is PATIENCE.

Remain calm if he mixes his mashes potatoes with his chocolate pudding, stirs his coffee with his finger, or eats as though someone was going to steal his food.

Bear with him if he walks out to the back patio and throws the trash over the railing into the backyard.

Do not be alarmed when he walks through a door and ducks his head and raises his feet, because it's not a neurotic condition. It's just the way he has been walking for the past 6 months.

Show no surprise if he accuses the grocer of being a thief, argues with the sales clerk about the price of each item, or tries to sell cigarettes to the newsboy on the sly.

Most important of all:

His digestive tract will also require some adjustment.

For the first week, all vegetables must be boiled until they are colorless and falling apart (after they have been sitting out in the hot sun for at least a week prior to his getting home).

Eggs must be tinged with a shade of green and be runny, bacon nearly raw and all other meats must be extremely well done.

Have beef for the first five or six days, calling it roast beef the first night, braised beef the second, beef tips the third, beef stew the fourth, etc.

If milk is served, it should be at room temperature and slightly diluted with water.

If he prefers to eat his meals while sitting next to the trash can, don't be concerned. He's grown so used to the smell that it may take a while for his normal tastes to return.

In the evenings, turn off all air-conditioning, open all windows and let in as many bugs as possible.

Let him sleep on the floor in the laundry room with the dirty clothes because he's so used to the smell.

For the first few nights, wake him every three or four hours. Tell him he's late for the night watch in the backyard. He'll understand because he's been doing something just as stupid for the past six months.

Under no circumstances should he be allowed to get a complete nights sleep during the critical adjustment time.

His daily routine may seem strange to you, especially when he wakes everyone up at six in the morning screaming "Reveille-Reveille, all hands heave out and trice up!" Just smile and nod and make sure everyone is up and on the back porch at seven for muster, instruction and inspection.

Then, in the late afternoon, humor him when he walks around the house closing all the windows and doors and reports to you that yoke is set throughout the house.

After sundown, don't argue with him when he yells at you for opening up the window blinds while darken house is set.

His language may seem foreign and you may not understand all the terms he uses. It isn't necessary that you do. Just smile and be pleasant. Some of the terms you may hear are Turn-to, Sweepers-Sweepers, Men working aloft, This is a drill, Wog, Beer-thirty, etc.

Do not be surprised when he answers the phone and instead of saying "Hello," he says: the room he's in, his rank and name. For example, Living Room, "You Fill in the Blank" speaking, this is a non-secured line subject to monitoring, how may I help you, Sir?

NEVER make favorable references to the Navy leadership structure. To do so will usually illicit an extremely loud and profane outburst which may continue for hours.

The bathroom is quite possibly the most dangerous place in the house for your USS Always Gone returnee. Before he arrives, strip the bathroom of all accessories such, bathmats and any and all toiletry items. Crack the mirror and run water on the floor. Toilet paper is optional, but if it is furnished, it must be placed in a puddle on the floor. Turn off the hot water at the source for the first few days. Wait until he is in the shower, soaped up and then turn the water off altogether for about 15 minutes. All of these precautions are imperative, because if he walks into a bathroom which is complete with the above mentioned items, he may shrink into a corner and curl up into a fetal position, wide-eyed and shaking. If this happens, there are only two proven and accepted methods of snapping him out of it; yell "Mail-Call or Liberty-Call." In either case, stay clear of the doorway.

In closing, always remember that beneath that suntanned shell there beats a heart of gold, it being the only thing the Navy couldn't confiscate or reschedule at a later date. With kindness, patience and the occasional swift kick, your loved one will soon return to his former self.

Barracks Inspection
By Author Unknown
Contributed by Donald Johnson

Having just joined my first command, I was assigned to the barracks and immediately put on cleaning duty. I had thought I did a good job of cleaning the room I was assigned to when I endured my first inspection at the hands of a new Ensign. The inspection was made and I was informed I had one hit. When I asked what the hit was I was told I had a suitcase stored under my rack and it was a fire hazard.

I asked if I could prove the suitcase was not a fire hazard would the hit be taken off the inspection report. I was told it was and I then informed the ensign I would need to use his phone to obtain the proof.

We then proceeded to his office, which he shared with the LCDR, and I made my phone call. The phone was answered and I asked to speak to Captain Monachino. When the captain got on the phone I said, "Dad, Is a suitcase stowed under a rack a fire hazard?" I was told not unless it contained Flammable Liquids or some other combustible material. I then handed the phone to the ensign for Dad to give the same information to the Ensign. The Ensign quickly sat at attention and said Yes Sir a lot. After saying goodbye, I was told the hit would be removed. I was then dismissed and as I was leaving the office the Ensign stopped me and asked me why I had not told him my father was a Captain. I then replied:

He's Captain of the fire department back home.

The LCDR fell out of his chair Laughing, The Ensign was not as amused and it took me 2 years to make E-4. I had to wait for the ensign to be transferred.

Chapter 3

Collision At Sea and More

Being at sea is as dangerous as flying or driving on California freeways. This chapter has two stories. One tells about a collision at sea while the other tells about the loss of a major shipboard asset.

> *"It was like riding over a piece of corrugated iron on a bicycle. There was a shuddering as we went over something and the initial reaction was, 'We've run aground!' Of course this was all split-second thinking, and then we realized we were in 1,100 fathoms of water so the chances of running aground were pretty slim. Another thought that went through our heads was that we'd hit a submarine because we knew there was a Russian submarine in the area monitoring the exercise."*
> —Petty Officer Ron Baker, HMAS Melbourne radio room operator after the HMAS Melbourne and USS Frank E Evans collision

On the morning of June 3, 1969, 74 American sailors died when the destroyer USS Frank E. Evans was cut in two by the HMAS Melbourne, an Australian aircraft carrier in the South China Sea.

Collision At Sea
By Les Bates

Little did we know when we set sail from San Diego, California on February 21, 1979 just how much our cruise would change during the course of our deployment to the Western Pacific. The USS Ranger (CV-61) stopped at Pearl Harbor, Hawaii and then pulled into Subic Bay in the Philippines. For the first 6 weeks or so, it was routine. The biggest disappointment thus far was the fact that we were not scheduled to visit any Japanese port during our six month cruise. Many people think that Japan is the nicest, friendliest, and the most worthwhile country to visit in the Far East.

In early April 1979 we set sail from Subic Bay, heading west/southwest toward the Straits of Malacca, on our way to the Indian Ocean. The Iranian crisis was still going on and the U.S. kept at least one aircraft carrier on station in the Indian Ocean ready to launch aircraft. The USS Midway (CV-41), homeported in Yokosuka, Japan, was on station and we were going to relieve her at the end of the week.

Sometime in the earl morning hours of April 5, 1979, the Ranger collided with a tanker called Fortune Monrovia. We were able to back out of there safely, and the tanker managed to stay afloat. There were no injuries on board our ship, but I heard that there was death on the tanker as well as a few injuries. We were extremely fortunate that no fire broke out. That could have been a disaster. We headed back to Subic Bay for temporary repairs, and then, to the joy of many of our crewmembers, we headed up to Yokosuka, Japan for additional temporary repairs and a lot of measuring, preliminary meetings, etc. for permanent repairs to be accomplished later on in the cruise. After ten days in a Yokosuka drydock, we left to continue our cruise as though nothing had happened.

However, the Ranger never was sent to the Indian Ocean. Our concrete bow made us only available for emergency duty. We spent the rest of our cruise patrolling the Sea of Japan and the South China Sea. We had port visits to Hong Kong, Pattaya Beach, Thailand and Pusan, Korea. Yokosuka, Japan was our unexpected bonus. Japan was not on our original schedule. We ended up having our cruise extended a month and returned to numerous areas of the country, sample the Japanese cuisine and lifestyle, and meet and create new friendships with the warm and wonderful people of Japan. We also had the opportunity to participate in the many athletic events that were offered at the sprawling American Naval Base at Yokosuka.

The collision did a lot more than just set us up to spend a lot of time in Japan. Three officers, our Commanding Officer, Ship's Navigator and the Officer-of-the-Deck (OOD), were relieved of duty. The naval careers were as good as over. Three other officers had to be ordered in to relieve these three, so other lives were badly interrupted. There was no other aircraft carrier that could immediately relieve the Midway, so guess who got to stay on station in the Indian Ocean for a few more weeks? There families and friends, who were in Yokosuka by the way, must have loved seeing all those Ranger sailors running around the base there.

Where's The Bow Ramp?
By Donald Johnson

I had never even thought about how a medium size Navy ship could lose something that weighs in at 38 tons. I had heard where ship's had lost anchors at sea because someone did not do their job or they decided to anchor in 35,000 feet of water like the Marianas Trench off Guam. But an LST's bow ramp? Let me tell you how that happened.

This particular deployment was the most messed up deployments I had would be on in my entire career. USS Peoria (LST-1183) deployed in April 1976 about 12 days after I re-enlisted after being out of the Navy for 2 ½ years. Our first stop was in Pearl Harbor where our ship's crew helped to clear out the Enlisted Club. I just happened to have duty that first night in port.

Our next stop was Guam for about a week to get some work done that was not completed in San Diego before we left. I also dropped off half my tele-type machines there on the first day in. We had about 300 Marines on board, too. Between the Marines and the ship's crew we cleared out the Enlisted Club there. It all started on a bus that four my radiomen and I had boarded to head back to the ship to prepare to get underway to evade a typhoon the next morning. I started the fight between two Marines and it snowballed from there. We were sitting in the back of the bus when about 20 Marines boarded. Two of them were arguing and one kept yelling that he was going to kick this other Marine's butt. That went on for about 10 minutes and I got tired of the mouth of the one Marine and I stood up and yelled, "If you are going to kick his butt, then kick it. Quit pussyfooting around and DO IT!" Then the loud mouth Marine hit the other Marine and now it was on. The next thing that happens is the Shore Patrol board the bus and spraying Mace all over the place. I got some in my eyes and decided this was not the place for me. I opened the back of the bus and fell out with my four buddies falling on top of me. We grabbed the first cab and got out of there. We got back to the ship and I went down to get dressed to go up to Radio to begin preps for getting underway.

The next day we left port to evade Super Typhoon Pamela. I wrote about riding out this typhoon in my first book entitled, "It Wasn't Just A Job; It Was An Adventure." We pulled back into Guam after a few days of riding out this super storm to find Guam completely devastated by the typhoon. We stayed for another six weeks to help restore power and water services and to help clean up the island.

Our next stop was Okinawa to drop the Marines off for training and would be back later to pick them up. We were only going to be in port over night. Once again the ship's crew cleared the Enlisted Club.

After Okinawa it was going to be a stop in Yokosuka, Japan and then Numazu, Japan and then Sasebo, Japan before heading to Subic Bay, Philippines and Sattahip, Thailand. We became a cargo carrier after dropping the Marines off.

Our stop in Yokosuka was uneventful. That was the first port that the ship's crew did not clear out the Enlisted Club. Most of us went out to the Haunch to drink and come back to the ship to sleep it off.

We were to drop off some Marine equipment at Numazu which was near the Marine Corp Base at Camp Fuji at the base of Mt. Fuji. Numazu had two or three sand piers jetting out into the water. As the ship neared the sand piers, the captain, Commander (Wild Bill) Bishop had the engineers open the bow doors so that they could slide the bow ramp out along its track. He had it lowered so that as we got to the pier they would be able to drop it down to offload the Marine equipment. They had lowered it too low and did not back off the engines soon enough and they hit the sand pier at 5 knots jamming the bow ramp into the sand pier and burning out the motor winches that operated the bow ramp.

We offloaded all of the Marine equipment and when it came time to leave they were trying to figure out how they were going to pull the bow ramp back into the ship. The motor winches were broken and could not pull the bow ramp. We were scheduled to be in Sasebo in three days and the captain did not want to be late for a scheduled cargo pickup. So he and his wardroom (officers) decided to depart with the bow ramp still hanging down. The ship looked like an old hound dog with his tongue hanging out and panting. Now it was time to figure out how they were going to pull the bow ramp back in.

As we were steaming at about 5 knots in northerly direction, the seas began to pick up. The captain was becoming worried because of the bow ramp. The very forward part of the ramp was about eight feet above the water. If the seas began to get worse and began to make swells of 4-6 feet that could cause a problem because the ship rolls and pitches. If it pitched too much forward, the waves could hit the bow ramp and cause it to fall into the ocean.

The first decision made was to attach some sturdy steel cable to two 10 ton motor winches near the aft flight deck and pull it back onboard that way. So they began the process to do that. They ran the cable fore and aft and hooked the cable to the winches and to a couple of strong points on the bow ramp. Then they began the process of starting the motor winches as many of us watched the bow ramp being pulled back on board. I was standing on the signal bridge watching everything going on with the operation when all of a sudden one of the cables breaks and acts like a whip and began to swing back and forth. The Chief Boatswains Mate that was supervising the operation did not get completely out of the way. The cable hit him in the hip and threw him up against an aluminum bulkhead. His hip was broken and he received other bumps and bruises. We now had to find a way to medevac him off the ship.

That bow ramp was still hanging down. We still had to get the bow ramp up or secure better so that it did not fall into the ocean. Since the 10 ton motor winches were not strong enough to pull the bow ramp back into the ship, they decided to secure the ramp with more strong steel cable. They had five men from the Deck Department on top of the bow ramp trying to secure it when all of a sudden a wave hit the bow ramp pretty much perpendicular causing the bow ramp to dip which caused the bow ramp cables that were still holding it in place to snap knocking the bow ramp into the ocean. The five sailors went overboard with the bow ramp.

Now it was "Man Overboard. This is not a drill." We dropped a motor whale boat into the water and picked them up in just a matter of minutes. All five of them had been injured to some extent. Now we had six men that needed to be medevaced. God was with us on this evolution, because luckily no one was killed.

We dropped a couple of floating buoys into the water as an indicator of the approximate position that the bow ramp was lost. Naval messages went out to all of the ship's chain of command letting them know about the accident. I took over the watch to ensure that the messages got out okay. I was also nosy and wanted to see what type of information they were passing up the chain.

A medevac helo was being sent from Yokosuka to pick up the injured sailors. It arrived a few hours later. We received a message stating that the USS Brunswick, a salvage ship, was on its way to help us locate the bow ramp.

The Brunswick arrived on scene a couple of days later. We stayed with them for the next week. Their divers had not found the bow ramp before we left.

The captain missed his port visit to Sasebo. We now headed for a few days in Subic before we headed to Sattahip to pick up some Army retrograde. The Army had just closed all of their operations down in Thailand and we were to pick up all of their equipment that they could not put on a plane.

After picking up the retrograde in Sattahip, we headed back to Subic to drop it off and then back to Yokosuka, if they found the bow ramp. By the time we pulled into Subic the Navy divers had not found the bow ramp. They were looking for it in about 300-400 feet of water. The Japanese government then offered their help with a new minesweeper that had a special sonar on board. When they got on the scene, they located the bow ramp in about two hours. The Brunswick divers tried for six weeks. They were mad as hell at us.

When we pulled back into Yokosuka to have the bow ramp placed back on board, we moored in front of the Brunswick. They had a big sign on the side of ship saying that we caused them six weeks of lost liberty. What a bunch of whiners! We did not spend too much time inport over this. The shipyard just placed it back into the tracks and pushed it back onto the ship. The shipyard in Subic would take care of all of the repairs. We would end up spending about three weeks in Subic.

This incident sparked a lot of interest from Congressmen. The two engineers who were brothers and who were operating the original bow ramp motor winches when the ship hit the sand pier at 5 knots sent a letter off explaining what had happened. Three of the six injured sailors also sent letters off to their Congressman. They all felt we had a dangerous situation from the time we hit the sand pier until the bow ramp fell into the ocean. An interior communications specialist from the Engineering Department was up on the signal bridge with me taking pictures of everything that had happened from the time we pulled away from the sand pier until we lost the bow ramp and the sailors overboard. His pictures were used as evidence in a hearing that happened as soon as we got back to San Diego. Commander Bishop was relieved not long after that.

Thirty-eight tons of aluminum lost at sea for six weeks. The Peoria sailors were talking about that deployment for a few years after that.

Chapter 4

World War II Experiences

This chapter includes a story I wrote about my uncle, Herb McElroy and two stories, which are the memoirs of my closest friend and confidante, Vern Bluhm.

> *"The battle of Iwo Jima has been won. Among the Americans who served on Iwo, uncommon valor was a common virtue."*
> —Fleet Admiral Chester W. Nimitz, 17 March 1945.

World War II Casualites—292,131 KIA, 115,185 non-combat related deaths, 670,846 Wounded

Uncle Herb Aboard The Makassar Strait
By Donald Johnson

My maternal uncle, Herb McElroy, served onboard USS Makassar Strait (CVE-91) shortly after it was commissioned (early 1944) to the end of the war (early to mid 1946). He advanced to YN2 or Yeoman Second Class Petty Officer. He decided to not make the Navy a career because he disliked the commissioned officer community. He felt they set themselves on a pedestal while looking down on the enlisted. He said that there were a few exceptions.

I had gone through his cruise book and found that he had been a member of a shipboard championship basketball team. That situation made me think back to when I coached a team of ragtag players on Adak to a second place finish in the league. We only lost two games and those were to the first place team which had some good former college basketball players.

Shipboard recreation had not really changed over the years. They had some of the same recreation during WWII that we had years later sitting off the coast of Vietnam or in the Persian Gulf.

I have talked to him a few times in the past few years to find out what had happened on the Makassar. He said they were never really in combat and was assigned to training air squadrons on take off and landing and as a medevac ship.

I did find out that the Makassar Strait did provide close-in ground support and combat air patrol over the main aircraft carrier battle groups off Okinawa. Those aircrews operated under the command of the commanding officer of the USS Saratoga (CV-3), Captain Cassidy, who was the commanding officer of my good friend Vern Bluhm. His story follows this story.

The information I have below was obtained from his cruise book and a few other places like Internet websites.

After shakedown in 1944 along the west coast, Makassar Strait departed San Diego 6 June and steamed via Pearl Harbor to the Marshalls carrying replacement aircraft and passengers; thence, she transported military casualties to Pearl Harbor and the west coast where she arrived in San Diego on 13 July.

During much of the next 2 months she trained carrier pilots off southern California. Between 25 September and 15 October she ferried 129 planes to Hawaii and to Manus, Admiralties. After returning to Pearl Harbor on 26 October with 70 damaged wildcats on board, she resumed pilot training operations out of Pearl Harbor.

During the next 3 months Makassar Strait rendered valuable service in the training of naval and marine aviators. Pilots from a dozen air groups and squadrons made more than 6,700 landings as she participated in combat air patrol and hunter-killer training exercises and night carrier operations, as well as defensive training against simulated bomb and torpedo attacks.

With Composite Squadron 97 embarked, Makassar Strait departed Pearl Harbor 29 January 1945 and steamed via Eniwetok for combat duty in the western Pacific. Assigned to TG 50.8, between 9 February and 8 April she protected logistics ships operating in support of the Fast Carrier Task Force during devastating air strikes against enemy targets from the Bonins to the Ryukus.

Assigned to a support carrier group on 8 April, Makassar Strait began air operations in the intense fighting on Okinawa. During the next 4 weeks she launched scores of sorties against targets in the Ryukus. Her planes provided close air support for American ground troops and struck with effective and devastating force against enemy gun emplacements, ground installations, and airfields as determined Americans drove to capture Okinawa—the enemy's last bastion of his crumbling empire. In addition the escort carrier's planes splashed four enemy aircraft.

Makassar Strait transferred her air squadron to Shipley Bay (CVE-85) at Kerama Retto on 7 May and departed later that day for Guam where she arrived on the 11th. She now operated in the Marianas between Guam and Saipan providing refresher training for carrier pilots, until departing for Hawaii on 19 July. Steaming via Kwajalein where she loaded 50 planes, she reached Pearl Harbor on 29 July. There she embarked 387 military passengers and sailed 14 August for the United States.

Arriving in San Diego on 21 August, Makassar Strait had steamed more than 91,000 miles in support of the Allied victory in the Pacific. She continued to train carrier pilots during the next 2 months; by the end of October the total number of landings on her flight deck since her commissioning had surpassed 15,500.

Makassar Strait departed San Diego 4 November for "Magic Carpet" duty. Steaming via Pearl Harbor, she transported replacement troops to the Marshalls; and after embarking 1,092 veterans at Kwajalein returned to San Diego on 29 November. Between 4 December and 3 January 1946 she made a similar cruise to Guam and back, transporting 1,123 officers and men to the United States.

Departing San Diego on 5 January, Makassar Strait steamed via San Francisco to Tacoma, Wash., where she arrived 12 January. Assigned to the 19th Fleet, she underwent deactivation and decommissioned 9 August 1946. She entered the Pacific Reserve Fleet at Tacoma; and, while berthed there, was reclassified CVU 91 on 12 June 1955. On 28 August 1958 the Secretary of' the Navy authorized her to be used as target to destruction. Her name was struck from the Navy list 1 September 1958. Makassar Strait received two battle stars for World War II service.

Life Aboard the Sara During WW II
By Vern Bluhm

I guess that the reason I joined the Navy was that I was raised in Bremerton, Washington where Puget Sound Naval Shipyard is located. From my house I could look down into the shipyard all the time. My Grandfather and Dad worked in Shop 56 in the shipyard.

I joined the Navy when I was 17 years and two days old on August 10, 1942. My birthday was on Saturday and I took my physical and oath on Monday, the 10th, and left the next day headed for boot camp in San Diego. My boot camp lasted for five weeks though originally it was suppose to be four weeks. Starting with my company, it was extended one week to give us some jujitsu (hand to hand) combat training. The island naval bases were being over run by the Japanese and the Navy had never trained their men in hand to hand fighting.

My boot camp training consisted of two afternoons of knot tying, on one afternoon we were in a pulling boat, one afternoon a Chief showed us how to field strip an M1 rifle, we never touched the rifle. That was our training except for the jujitsu training. The rest of the time we just marched. To be fair I have to say that nobody knew what to do with a mass of men that were coming into the military. It took time to get things organized.

After boot camp I was given one week of leave, and we were the last company to get that. I took a Greyhound bus from San Diego to Seattle. Everyone on that bus was a sailor heading for Seattle, or near by areas, on boot leave, except one married civilian woman. Never did one woman have so many servants. We made that trip in record time.

After the leave I headed back to San Diego to ship out. They put us on a train for San Francisco, and it took us five day to reach San Diego. They moved us all over the state so that any spies would not know where we were going or so they told us. I believe that they felt it was necessary. When we arrived in San Francisco it was late in the evening and we were bussed to Treasure Island which the Navy had taken over. We thought we would have to wait until morning to eat, but when they offloaded us from the busses it was at the chow hall and they had a spread that was unbelievable. There were several kinds of meat and chicken, potatoes, several kinds vegetables, and a half a dozen kinds of deserts. Never, after that did I eat that good in the Navy.

The ship that we shipped out on for Pearl Harbor was the USS Republic. It was a German liner that had been confiscated in New York harbor when the U.S. declared war on Germany. It took us 11 days to get to Pearl. The bunks were so close together that you had to slide into yours on your back, and if wanted to turn over, you had to get out and slide in on your stomach. We carried a very special human manifest, forty prostitutes for the houses in Honolulu. Before Eleanor Roosevelt got wind of it, the Navy had several houses of ill repute that they kept staffed. I know this as a fact as we were assigned to guard duty around the area that they lived in. Some of the woman would come out to talk to us. One told me that they had to promise, in writing, that one, they would be subject to medical tests every other week, and two, that they would not try to rip the servicemen off since their prices would be set by the Navy, and three, that they would not try to marry any of the servicemen. Before this practice is condemned too harshly, people must realize that when this practice was stopped VD went up 100% and it remained a problem as long as I was in the Navy.

When we arrived in the Hawaiian Islands, they would not let us come into Pearl Harbor as there was not much cleaned up, and they were very busy with salvage operations. We off-loaded in Honolulu at the Aloha Tower. We were taken by a small train called "the pineapple express" to Ford Island in Pearl. The train tracks ran behind the pineapple warehouses, and as we passed, people stood out on the loading dock and tossed pineapples to us, my first taste of fresh pineapple off the plant. When we arrived at Pearl, we were in a holding pool called FFT (For Further Transfer). One Tuesday we all were told that we had to fall out on the baseball field early in the morning. The rumor was that we were shipping out. I stood out there all day and my name was never called, along with three other sailors. The Chief in Charge ask us what we were waiting for. We told him our names had not been called. He looked on his list and sure enough there were no check marks by our names. He told us OK he had a carrier, two tin cans, and a cruiser. He told me that because my name started with a "B" I could have the first choice. I asked the name of the carrier and he told me the "Sara" (USS Saratoga CV-3). I told him that I would take it because I knew, or was pretty sure, that it would go back to Bremerton when it went stateside. That was on October 27, 1942. The old Navy Day. That was when each service had their day.

When I reported aboard the Sara, I was amazed. I had never been on her when she was in Bremerton. I know that she was big but I had no idea how big it was. I found it almost impossible to believe that it would float. At first I was assigned to the radio shack. That was a mistake. No matter how hard I tried, I could not get Morse code. It took my Chief and Officer about a month to find this out and I was transferred to the deck force. I spent just a short time in the deck force when an opportunity came for me to apply for radar operator school.

Let me give you some idea of what Oahu Island and Honolulu was like at that time. Except for the towns and the cities, Oahu was one large military camp. Part of Honolulu fit that description also. Honolulu before the war was not a very large city. Its streets in the downtown area were rather narrow. Everywhere you went there were men and woman in uniform. It was rare to see people in civilian cloths on the streets. The congestion was immense. In the downtown area of Front Street it was nearly impossible to walk on the sidewalk. There just was not room. Everywhere you went there were lines and crowds of humanity. There were uniforms of every Allied nation. There was still much war damage in Pearl. None of the ships that had been sunk were raised. There were wrecks of buildings, ships and aircraft everywhere. Oahu Island was to remain like this for many months, until the war moved much further to the northwest. As the war moved on the congestion became less and less.

Unless you were fortunate to be invited to a private home, as I was, then you had put up with the crowds. Grandpa Bluhm had a cousin living in Honolulu. His name was Ray Harris. Ray was a retired Navy Chief Warrant Pharmacist. During his time in the Navy Ray had become interested in sea shells. There is a name for this specialty but do not ask me what it is. He was the head of a department when I first met him at the Bishop Museum in Honolulu. Ray later became the museum's curator. Ray wanted me to bring him back bags of sand from wherever I went, and he wanted me to have the map position put on the bags. I told him that I could not do that as it would show where the ship had been and that was classified. He contacted the ships XO and cleared with him that in this case it would be OK.

I left off with me going to radar school. After radar school I returned to the Sara. When I went onboard the Sara, she was in drydock because she had got a torpedo off of Midway Island. Then we sailed for the South Pacific. But first let me try and describe the Sara. At the hull she was 888' long. At the flight deck she was 918' long. from the flight deck to the top of the mainmast was 150'. From the edge of the flight deck to the water line was 60' and from the water line to the bottom of the keel was 37". she had a wartime crew of 2700 men including the aircrew. She carried 101 aircraft. Fighters (F4F and later F6F), torpedo bombers (STB and later TBF) and Douglas Dauntless dive bombers (SBD). At that time the Saratoga and the Lexington (sister ship to the Sara) were the largest ships afloat, of any nation. Later the Lex was lost at the Battle of the Coral Sea. The only ship close, in size, to the Sara and Lex was the French battleship Richelieu. When we left Pearl, we headed in the general direction of southwest. I say general because we almost always traveled on a zigzag course. The first stop was Suva, Fiji. Suva was a place out of a travel book. One of the things that I remember was that we had to lay at anchor outside of the harbor for Suva did not have a dock or pier big enough for us and the harbor was too shallow. In many cases when we were not underway, there would be steel net surrounding us in case a sub tried to torpedo us. These nets would be held in place by buoys. While at anchor in Suva, we had such a net surrounding us and we would go swimming after duty hours. There were sharks in the waters so we had Marine sharpshooters with M1 rifles standing on the flight deck to shoot any shark that was nosing around. When we left Suva the next stop was Noumea, New Caledonia. We pulled into Noumea on Christmas day 1942. The first thing that I noticed about Noumea was the water. To get to the harbor of Noumea you had to go through a barrier reef. I could stand on the flight deck and look down and see the white sand on the bottom. This was to prove to be our "home port" for about eighteen months. Our task force, the Sara, two Anti Aircraft (AA) cruisers the San Juan and the San Diego, three tin cans the Dunlop, Fanning, and Cummings were suppose to stop the Japanese fleet if they headed for Australia. It was to be nearly nine months before we saw another ship of the line flying the American flag. When we got to Noumea they outfitted some of the dive bombers with radar. They did not have any aircrew trained to operate them so they took shipboard operators, in particular, me, and said you are now flying radarmen. No orders were ever cut; it was all VOCO (Verbal Order Of Commanding Officer). We were still considered part of the ship's crew but flew all the time. In the mean time we were suppose to support the Marines with air power on Guadalcanal. Like all gravel agitators of that time the Marines were never taught how to control aircraft and they would either pull our bombs down on top of themselves or they were having them drop their bombs too far out. The pilots were very unhappy about this situation. They were risking there lives and being very ineffective. So our skipper, Captain John H. Cassidy suggested to Marine BG Vanderbilt, CO of the 1st Marine Div. on Guadalcanal, that he send a team of officers and men to control the aircraft. I was one of the people selected.

The length of our time on Guadalcanal was supposed to only last until they had secured the airfield that was later to be named Henderson Field. It turned out that we, the team, did such a good job that after the airfield was secured that Vanderbilt would not let us return. We were on the "Canal" for three months. The Navy and the Marines were supposed to be at each others throats all the time and sometimes they were. But never could anyone have been better treated than the way the Marines treated us. Those of us designated to carry the radios were carrying the old-fashioned field radio packs. These radios weighed 90 pounds. They were so large and cumbersome that we could not carry side arms. Each of us had two Marines assigned to do nothing but protect us. I actually heard Gen. Vanderbilt tell the Marines that their only job was to stand between any bullet and us. How is that for an assignment? After we did get back to the ship I had a far different view and respect for the Marines.

It might be of some value for me to tell you of a typical day on the Sara at sea. The Ship ran on four hour watches. Besides your watch station you had your regular duty station hours that you normally worked from 8AM-4PM unless you were part of the flight crews. They had their own schedules. The only exception to this was that if you had the mid-watch you got to sleep in until 10AM or if you had the dog watch, 4PM-6PM you were allowed to leave your work station at 2PM. Every morning and every evening there was General Quarters (GQ). They always started one half hour before sunrise until one half hour after sunrise and the same way for the evening. At dawn aircraft patrols were launched just after/before GQ. We always had two types of patrols aloft from the dawn patrol until just before dark. These patrols amounted to about a total of 12 aircraft at a time and would last for about three hours. One was the Antisubmarine Patrols (ASP) made up of TBFs and SBDs. The Combat Air Patrol (CAP) was made up of F4/6Fs

Before I go any further I would like to quash a popular misconception. There is nothing glamorous about war! If I had to choose one word to describe war, it would be BORING. War is a LOT of waiting. During WWII in the Navy you did the same routine day after day after day until you did your routine like a bunch of zombies. For the Army and the Marines that single word was TIRED! They never got the rest the needed day or night. There is nothing glamorous about men getting killed or being blow apart. I have said many times, and I still believe it, that I do not know and/or have read about very few Admirals or Generals that would not be willing to be put out a job if peace would descend all over the earth. The one exception to this would be the Pattons and they never minimized the dirty parts of war; besides they were few and far between. Now I will get off my soap box.

After the Marines had the upper hand on the "Canal", the Sara was assigned other targets such as Bougainville on Vella Lavella Island and Espirito Santo (land of the spirit). Three Islands made up Espirito Santo, one French and two British. Did you every try standing at attention and salute through God Save the King, Marseillaise, and the Star Spangled Banner every morning for three weeks? I did.

One of the raids that the Sara was in on was the first raid of Rabaul on New Britain Island. This raid was to have a very strange twist many years later. Rabaul was a very large Japanese base with several airfields and a large harbor. The harbor had a large barrier reef around the harbor. When the Japanese decided to build the harbor, they blew a passage through the reef. They made the mistake in making the passage narrow thinking that it would be easier to defend. We were the first ship to raid Rabaul and the Japanese thought it was too strong for a carrier to attack. As usual we launched our strike force with every plane that we could, except the ASP and CAP. The Captain dared to get as close as he could. The strike was launched about an hour before dawn so that they would arrive about daybreak. As we flew toward Rabaul the Sara turned and headed back away from the launch point. This was SOP (Standard Operating Procedure) so that they would be at the recovery point when the planes returned. The recovery point was the furthermost point that the planes could fly even if it was damaged. When we got to Rabaul, the Japanese had no idea that we were anywhere within a thousand miles of them. They honestly felt that we did not have the capability to raid them. The Japanese underestimated the U.S. many times in the next three years. Another problem they had was that they had very poor radar. The first ship hit was a tin can that was coming into the harbor. It was sunk in the reef passageway bottling up the rest of the fleet. From then on it was like shooting fish in a barrel. My plane was diving on a light cruiser when there was huge, load noise. Water flew into the air with a lot of other stuff. After it settled down we saw only open water where there once was a heavy cruiser. During the debriefing every one figured that one of the dive bombers that had released the bomb got real lucky and dropped it down the stack. It went off inside the ship and broke her back, and she went down in less than a couple minutes with all hands aboard. Now for the twist…Years later, after I retired, Frieda and I were watching Jacque Cousteau and the program was about them diving down to that Japanese heavy cruiser, and the other ships that we had put down on the bottom of Rabaul harbor. They showed that in fact a bomb had broken the cruiser's back.

While the Sara was in Noumea we were involved in many raids on the Japanese held territory beside the Canal. As the Marines, and later the Army, secured the Canal we were given targets further away from Noumea.

Before I get too much further I would like to describe New Caledonia. During the early part of the war, the Saturday Evening Post magazine had an article about Noumea and described it as, "Hell on a swing shift." Before the war Noumea was a French penal colony. This is where France sent their political prisoners. The natives were cannibals until just before the war and the French had a leper colony there. When the war came along, they just let all the political prisoners go which was very typical of the French. In short order New Caledonia became one huge Marine base with a few other entities thrown in such as Admiral "Bull" Halsey's HQ, a very large supply depot, and thereby hangs a tale.

I was suppose to be on liberty one day and was just hanging around. If you had been in Noumea three times, you saw everything that there was to see. LCDR John Halsey Jr., the Admiral's son, was on the Sara as a supply officer. I knew John Halsey quite well. I ran across him on the ship one day and remarked that I had liberty but there was nothing that I wanted to return to Noumea for or words to that effect. John Jr. asked if I would mind giving him a hand taking some paper work and other material over to the beach. I had nothing else to do so I said I would. After we got through at the depot, John remarked that he was going to see his Dad. I told him that I would go back to the landing and get a boat back to the ship. We were anchored in the harbor. John would not hear of it. I had to come with him. So being a good Seaman 1/c I tagged along. On our way to the Admiral's office, we passed LTs, LCDRs, Commanders and the Admiral's Chief of Staff who was a Captain. John asked if his Dad was busy and the Captain said, "No, go on in." John motioned for me to follow.

Let me try to describe what I saw when the door opened. The room was not too large. There was a desk, chair, flag, and off to one side a small conference table with chairs with a few pictures on the wall. He had a picture of the Sara which he once commanded. The Admiral had his feet up on the desk and he was leaning back in his chair. His uniform looked like he had slept in it for a week, and it could have been that long that he had worn that uniform. When the door opened, he looked up and saw John. He tossed the papers he was reading at the desk. Part of them landed on the desk and part on the floor. I still do not know to this day how he could have found anything on that desk. It was a mess. When he saw that it was his son, he got up and let out a big, "JOHN!", got up, came over and gave him a big hug. In the meantime, I, that poor Seaman 1/c, did not know what to do so I stood just inside the door. The Admiral while talking to his son would look around at me and then go on talking. After this happened two or three times I could just see me being a Seaman for the rest of my life while in the brig. Finally the Admiral said; "Who in the Hell is that?" John told him, "Dad, this is Seaman Bluhm from the ship. He helped take some stuff ashore." The Admiral's response was, "God damn it son, don't just stand there come over here!" I had lunch with the Admiral and John Jr.

People have asked me how I felt during the first combat that I was in. The Sara was never hit after The Battle of Midway until very late in the war. My first taste of combat came on the "Canal." How did I feel? I was close to petrified. The only thing that kept me going was that I knew that others were depending on me. You must remember that I was seventeen and I never had a person try to kill me. Those of us packing the radios were favorite targets of the snipers because we were the people that controlled the airplanes. The most helpless feeling was being in a bunker and being shelled by the Japanese warship. They would pound us for hours, night after night, with everything from 5".38MM to 18" or their equivalent. There was nothing you could do but sit there and take it. We were too scared to even talk. I saw men with many years in the military crack during the shelling. Why not me? To this day I do not know. Maybe it was that I did not have enough sense to be that scared. There is no way that you can describe the absolute terror that a person feels in combat. When it is all over, you feel immense relief that you are still alive and COMPLETELY drained of all other feelings and strength. I guess that is about as close as I can come to answering people's questions about combat.

I never had similar feelings when the ship was attacked by Japanese planes. One, you were too busy to think about being scared. Two, even after the attacking planes left you never relaxed. You were always concerned that there might be more planes. I was very lucky I never had to bail out of a plane. I had the same pilot all during the war. We did lose one plane and that was much later.

After the first raid on Rabaul we went back two other times. There was very little left after the third raid. Rabaul ceased to be a threat. Rabaul was never invaded. We just by passed it. The next major action that the Sara was involved in was the Gilbert Islands, especially Tarawa.

Tarawa was hell for the Marines, even more so than the "Canal." Over a period of three days the Marines and Army had 1,500 casualties. The casualties were primarily due to the fact that many of the landing craft got hung up on the reef because they made the initial lading at low tide. People should not be too hard on the high command because it is necessary to remember at this time, November of 1943, they were still developing amphibious warfare. The Japanese were really dug in. They had twenty years to fortify the island. I had a Marine tell me that the island was so honeycombed that when you dropped a grenade in a foxhole you would see the puff of smoke come up ten feet away. When we first went over the island to support the landings, the island was covered with palm trees. Before it was over there was not a tree with the top left on it. It was like a bunch of spires sticking up in the air. Of the 4,800 Japanese forces on the island at the start of the landings only 17 wounded Japanese soldiers were captured. None gave up. After Tarawa was secured we headed home.

Let me take time to explain a few things about carrier operations. Like with the USAF every plane had a crew chief. It was the responsibility of the man to see that his plane was mechanically in shape and ready to go for every scheduled flight. This was no small job. This meant that he had to work with the refuelers, the armors, radio repair, sheet metal workers, or whoever it required to make sure his plane was ready. He may have to replenish the oxygen. He would have to tape the muzzles of the guns so dirt could not be blown into the gun. One thing that most people did not realize about WW II carrier planes was why the nose stuck up in the air so high, and there was a very good reason for this. The reason was two fold; one was so that when they landed and the tail hook caught the arresting gear, the nose always comes down and the prop would not dig in to the deck. Second, so that if a person was caught in the slip stream of another plane, he could drop and be blown under the prop and not be hit by the prop and be killed.

There is a sea story about a young pilot. A brand-new ensign came aboard right out of flight school and started throwing his weight around. Soon everyone on the flight deck hated his guts. It got to the place where it was unsafe for him to be on the flight deck at night. The chief of the flight deck took the young man aside and told him that it was not the place of the chief to tell the ensign how to be an officer, but he did want to remind him that the men on the flight deck had to get him off but they did not have to get him back. The message got home load and clear. He changed over night.

The air crew was always briefed about an hour before flight time and this would depend on the kind of flight. This briefing would cover such things as targets/patrol areas, secondary targets, altitudes, flight plans to and from the targets, expected opposition. The briefing covered everything that pilots needed to know. The flight crews received their briefings separately from the pilots. The crew's briefing was much shorter, but once airborne the pilot usually shared what he was told with his crew. Shortly before the Battle of the Gilbert Islands, we had an addition to our task force that was the medium size carrier the USS Midway which was the first carrier that we operated with. After the Gilbert Islands were secured we were ordered to Bremerton for overhaul. This happened about every six months thereafter. I had been away from home a little over two years. I was looking forward to being able to get home. When we started for Bremerton, via Pearl, our task force tried to keep up with us until a couple of the tin cans (destroyers) burned out. Captain Cassidy told the rest of the task force to make their best time and that we would meet them in Pearl. This was not as foolhardy as it might seem as we could travel at 20-25 knots and the fastest sub could only do about 14 knots on the surface and about ten knots submerged. We always had our ASP and CAP up during all daylight hours. When we arrived in Pearl, we offloaded most of our ammo, aviation fuel, and stores. We did this in record time, about 72 hours. We were in Bremerton for about 30 days.

I think that I have been remiss for not giving a short history of the Sara. The ships that were to become the Sara and Lex were originally to be super dreadnoughts (battleships), and the keels were laid in 1917. Then in 1922 came the London Naval Agreement that said that no country would have dreadnoughts. Here the US had the keel laid and the hull built for two dreadnoughts. So they decided to make carriers out of them by just putting a flight deck on the hulls. All construction was done with rivets as welding had not been developed at that time. The rivet heads were about 1" in diameter. They were very well built ships. The Navy already had the USS Langley, a coaler that they had converted to a carrier and it was designated CV1 (designation for a carrier). The Lex was to become CV2 and the Sara CV3. They were the only carriers of any nation that had twin screws. Even the carriers of today have single screws. Each ship had 18 fire rooms. Their best speed was about 25 knots and for those days that was fast. All through WWII we continually could out run our escorts. Even when they had developed tin cans that would go 30-40 knots, they could not do that speed for a sustained period of time where we could go on and on.

After we left Bremerton we headed for Pearl again. Every time an air group has been inactive for a period of time, they have to be re-qualified on carrier landings. It is no small task to land on a carrier. This is what it is like to land on a carrier. You have the ship going into the wind, moving through the water at about 20 knots and pitching and rolling with the waves. That flight deck is moving up and down and rolling from side to side no matter how calm the ocean is. You have an airplane flying at 90-110 mph trying to catch the ship. It must be at just the right moment to catch a 1 1/4" cable stretched across the flight deck with a hook that is on the under side of the tail. It is not easy under the very best of the conditions, and the conditions are very seldom ideal. When a sailor says the ocean is calm, he means that it is not rolling as much as other times.

After leaving Pearl our first major operation was the Marshall Islands invasion. Eniwetok was the major battle. The one thing I always found astounding was how often planes would come back with their guns still taped. Contrary to the movies every time a plane took off, you did not always find a target worth shooting at. Most of the times the fighter would support the Army/Marines with strafing runs. As an operation progressed, the targets for the aircraft became less and less. From then on it was up the gravel agitators.

I think that this is the point that something should be said about the Army's roll in the South Pacific. I have felt for some years that the Army had gotten a bad rap. During the first part of the war, the Army's record was not very good for two basic reasons. First, the Army was never trained for amphibious warfare, and the Marines were. Second, the Army for the most part were never trained for jungle fighting, and again the Marines were. I feel that this lack of proper training was why the Army showed up so poor and had such high casualties. At the beginning of the war the Army Brass could not see any difference in fighting in Europe and the South Pacific. I have read where some of the comments of the Army officers of that time on this subject and have wondered how it was possible to be so stupid. Basically it is the difference of being able to seeing for yards or a few feet.

After the Marshall Islands we were detached from the U.S. fleet and sent to join with the British Seventh Far Eastern Fleet. Why should the Sara be operating with the British? I think it was just to show a sense of cooperation, and goodwill. We had our normal support group with us on this trip. We sailed down through the Tasman Sea. This was where we ran into the worse storm that I have ever been except one when I was in the Coast Guard. As I have said before, it was 60' from the top of the flight deck to the water line, and the flight deck was 918' long. We had white water rolling half way down the flight deck. When it can do that, it is some storm. It is my understanding from talking to the ship's captains that the Tasman Sea is considered the roughest stretch of water in the world. All the storms come right out of the Antarctica, and it is not all that far to the South Pole from Southern Australia. We pulled into the harbor of Hobart, Tasmania. We were there only two days. If we had one million pounds fresh out of the King's mint, it would not be worth the paper it was printed on. One of the first things that we sailors noticed was that everything was run by women. There were almost no men of military age left in Hobart. We were the largest ship of any nation to ever visit Hobart. They declared a one day holiday. We were being asked by the people of Hobart to two and three meals an evening. When we left Hobart we went to Perth and Fremantle, Australia. We stayed there for three weeks.

When we left Fremantle, we headed for Tincomalee, Ceylon (now Sri Lanka). We arrived in Tincomalee with much fanfare. We made several small raids with the British 7th Far Eastern Fleet. The two most important raids that we made were on Sabang, an island at the NW end of the Island of Sumatra, and Surabaya on the Island of Java. Sabang was important because it was a small Japanese naval base and air base, and was the HQ of the Japanese commander in that area. The mission was: 1) to destroy as much shipping as possible and destroy as many of the of the runways and aircraft as possible, 2) to have every plane strafe the HQ building where the Japanese Admiral stayed.

The plane that I was in made our dive and instead of climbing back up as was the norm we flattened out at the end of the dive and strafed as we flew across the field. The pilot would catch every thing in front and I would strafe the targets to the sides. Of course we strafed the HQ building. Just as we passed over the building the plane gave a lurch and there was a big bang. I thought that we had caught some flack. From where I was sitting I could not see any damage. One thing different about the Douglas Dive Bomber (SBD) was that you could fly it from the rear cockpit as well as the front cockpit. When airborne, I did get to fly the plane often. I kept watching the gages to watch for any hint of trouble. Everything was purring along just fine. We got back to the ship alright. After landing and securing the plane I got out and ducked under the plane to see what the damage was. That goofy pilot had raked the plane over the roof of the HQ building and we had stayed airborne. The pilot was John "Whitey" Welch from Greensboro, NC. Every time we went after a sea target he tried to play submarine and every time we went after a land target he tried to play groundhog. But given the choice I would not have had a different pilot. Whitey was a Fighter Direction Officer (FDO) and as such was considered part of the Combat Information Center team as I was. But both of us had more hours flying than in CIC.

The other raid was on Surabaya. This one was a big one. The aircraft carrier, HMS Illustrious was part of the British fleet. For the most part Sabang was a cake walk, but Surabaya was to be something all together different. We had to fly in from the South because the Java Sea is too confining an area. The shortest way was over three Japanese airfields. We were not too concerned about going in as we could fly in the dark and be flying high. We would hit the target at dawn but coming back would be a different story. As I had written earlier the Japanese radar was of a very poor quality so we did not feel that would cause problems. Also, the Japanese commanders, for the most part, did not believe in radar. What made Surabaya so important was That it was a very good port and it was an oil refinery city. We hit the targets just as planned. We were told that when we formed up for the return flight we were to fly back to the ship at tree top level. At each one of those fields we caught them napping and destroyed many aircraft. We were unbelievably lucky.

Back to Colombo we went. We operated with the British for a period of three months. Most of the time we were in port. We always had a group of British sailors on our ship after hours and on weekends. I was invited over to the HMS Warspite. The Warspite had spent over a year in Bremerton being repaired for battle damage before we entered the war. I was treated like a long lost brother. This is where I developed a love for Jamaican rum.

Mom had been after me for sometime to bring something back from the South Pacific. I tried to tell her that I was not at any place that I could get anything. Her answer was always, "I do not care if it is just a rock from the beach." This had been going on for sometime. One day when I was on liberty in Colombo I was walking by a small shop and saw some precious stones in the window. I went in and asked about them. There were two blue sapphires. They were cut in the long cut and I have forgot what the cut is called. After quite a few cups of tea the shopkeeper asked what I was going to do with the stones. I told him that I was going to give them to my Mother. He got up and went to the back of the shop. After a while he came out with an envelope and handed it to me and in it was a half a dozen ruby and diamond chips. When I had first asked about the stones, the shopkeeper had told me that one of them had a single flaw in it and he showed me where it was, right across the center. He suggested that the stone could be broken and re-cut for a ring. When I got back to Bremerton, I took the stones home. They were in a very nondescript box. I handed the box to Mom and told her; "Here are your stones. Now get off my back." Needless to say she was speechless when she opened the box. Mom had the good sapphire made into a necklace and the other stone was made into a ring. I do not remember what they cost, but they were dirt cheap, even for those days.

Just before we got ready to return to the Pacific, we had Lord Louis Mountbatten, the Allied Commander of the China/Burma Theater on board. I have often said that the higher a man goes in the military the more likable he is. It has been my experience that this was true. Yes, there are exceptions. Bull Halsey and Lord Louis were not an exception. When Lord Louis came on board the whole ship was in formation. They had built a podium and we were in a U formation around the podium. Captain Cassidy and Lord Louis came out. The Captain said a few words and turned the mike over to Lord Louis. The first thing he did was tell us to break ranks and come close. He had some of the Chiefs sitting on the edge of the podium. His excuse was that he did not have a loud voice. Yeah, an Admiral in the British Navy who did not develop a loud voice? Sure! He spoke for a few minutes thanking us for helping in that theater. Then he put his hand on a couple of Chiefs shoulders and stepped out in the crowd and went around shaking hands and thanking the crew. The British stock went up that day with our crew. He did this for almost an hour. I was one of the people that he shook hands with. He asked me where I was from. When I told him Bremerton, Washington, he told me; "Ah yes, I remember being there when I was a Midshipman," or words to that effect. How long ago do you think it was that he was a Midshipman?

When we left Colombo, we headed for Fremantle again and spent a week. I have a cute story about Fremantle. The first time we were there I met a girl and had asked her for a date that Saturday. When I arrived at her house, I was invited in. I talked to her Mom for awhile then we took off. As we were leaving, her Mom told me, "Now don't knock her up." I stopped dead in my tracks and the girl started laughing. Grabbing my arm and pulling me outside, she told me that was the way the Australians say, "Don't tire a person out." That sure was a different way of using that phrase.

From Fremantle we went onto Sidney. We were in Sidney for five days and then home again. When we left Sidney the Captain told our escorts to form up together and make their best time to Pearl. We took off by ourselves. The only time that we slowed down was to empty a tanker that had come out from Noumea, and then on to Pearl and then home.

Whenever we were in Bremerton, I would always sign up for the second leave party. I could stand on the flight deck and see the house. I would take leave and spend a week or two in Republic at Grandma and Grandpa's ranch. It was a chance for me to get away from it all and relax. It always did me wonders. Besides, I was home every night that I had liberty.

While in Bremerton, things happened. When we were in Bremerton, it seemed that Dad got the Sara. Though he professed to hate that ship, I think it was his doing. On one of the trips into homeport, I was mess cooking in the Chiefs quarters. I had got permission from the Chief in charge of the mess to bring in my Dad for coffee anytime after meals but only Dad. As usual when I was not doing any thing I would be asleep on a couch, any where. This day Dad had come up to get coffee and gab and I was asleep. When I woke up one of the Chiefs told me that Dad had been there, so I went where I knew that Dad's crew was working. I found the crew and asked where Earl Bluhm was. One of the men pointed down into the void. I went over to the manhole and I could see Dad hunkered down looking at something. Not far away was a 36" pipe wrench lying on the deck. I went over and picked it up and started beating on the deck above Dad's head. You could see by the looks on the faces of Dad's crew that they wondered if this sailor had lost his mind because not one of them knew me from Adam. Dad came barreling out of the manhole using every swear word he knew and believe me he knew a few. When he got out, he looked around to see who the nut was. I was standing there with the pipe wrench in my hand. Dad asked what I had done that for. I told him that I found out that he had come up to the mess for coffee and I came down to see if he still wanted some. He told me later that his ears had rung for an hour afterward.

The other story was about Mom. Mom and I had been downtown. I found out later that some of the men from my division had seen me with Mom. When I went back to the ship, they started razzing me about the "mature dates" that I was having. I tried to tell them that it was my Mother, but you know how that statement was accepted. One of the guys was doing most the talking. I bet him $10 that it was my Mother. He called me so I gave him our address and forgot about it. The next day the door bell rang. I went and answered it and here was this guy and two others from the ship. I invited them in and called, "Mom, will you come here for a minute?" When Mom came, the fellow that had called me never said a word. He took ten dollars out of his wallet and turned and left. Of course Mom wanted to know what that was all about. For years afterwards we laughed about that. What the guys did not take into consideration was that we were all dark from spending so much time in the tropics, where Mom was fair. There was more times that one that Mom would introduce me to some friend and they would look at her as to say what are you trying to pull?

After we left Bremerton we again qualified an air group and then headed out to the war again. We wound up in Ulithi Atoll. Ulithi Atoll is a group of islands that form a circle in the Pacific Ocean, but they are no "pearls of the Pacific." When we pulled in, there were more ships there than I had ever seen in one spot in my life. You name it and it was there. What we found out much later was that we were going to raid the main land of Japan. One of the little islands was called Mog Mog. This island was fairly round with all the land sloping up to the center with a flat top. There was about six palm trees on the island and nothing else. I would guess that it was about an eighth of a mile across. This was the recreation area for our ship. Each crew member was allowed to go over once every fourth day. They did have a crude baseball diamond and you were given two bottles of warm green beer and I mean green. It was in a clear white bottle so we saw how green it was. I forgot the name of the brewery, but I do remember it was bottled in San Jose, CA.

Over a period of a week all the ships in Ulithi headed north. We massed off the coast of Japan. In that task force there were a thousand ships of the line. I flew on three raids. After taking off all you could see were allied ships as far as the eye could see. Japan really got pounded because of the bombing that the B-29s were doing. These raids lasted for about three weeks.

Around the middle of February 1945, the Sara was detached and ordered to form up with, and become the "flag", of a task force of small "jeep" carriers supporting the Marines on Iwo Jima. To give you some idea of what the Marines were going through we had a "shirt-tail relation" that was in the initial landing at Iwo as a Marine Corporal. In forty-five minutes he was the company commander. We had been at Iwo about three days when on the evening of February 21, 1945 we were hit by five Japanese kamikaze planes and seven bombs. The attack lasted over a period from 5:05 PM until about 3:00 AM the next morning. We sailed away at eighteen knots with a three degree starboard list. Of the approximately 2700 men, there were 127 dead and missing with about 300 wounded. This was a small casualty list considering the confined space we were in.

The primary reason that we survived was that the Sara was a tight, well-disciplined, well-trained ship. We never left the ship without being inspected, even if we were going ashore in the islands in dungarees. You never saw a Sara sailor going ashore in a dirty uniform. Discipline and training is what put out the massive fire so quickly and it was what kept her afloat. I have heard that no other ship during the war sustained as much damage and remained afloat and I believe it. The Sara is where I developed my strong belief in discipline that lasted the rest of my military career.

On the way to Eniwetok we took care of our dead and wounded and did what we could to make the ship shipshape. Upon our arrival at Eniwetok we began to really look at our damage. Many pictures were taken of our damage, three footlockers full. The pictures and the ship's First Lieutenant who was the officer responsible for keeping the ship seaworthy were flown to Bremerton. At Eniwetok we offloaded our more seriously wounded to the base hospital, and then onto Pearl. On the way to Pearl we were involved in the search for General Doolittle. At Pearl we had many visitors to come aboard and look at the battle damage. Many of the visitors were pilots of the Army Air Corp that had flown by us during the search for Doolittle.

Upon our arrival in Bremerton we went immediately into drydock. On the pier along the side of the drydock were prefabricated parts waiting for us. It was one of the biggest prefabricated repair jobs done during the war. We were in Bremerton for forty-five days. Dad was one of the first shipyard workers onboard. He had not told Mom about how badly we had been damaged as he had no way of knowing if I was alive or dead.

After Bremerton we headed for Pearl. We never returned to the war zone again. We spent the rest of the war qualifying pilots in carrier landings. We were in Pearl when the word came that the Japanese have given up. We were tied up at berth 3, our normal place when we got the word. I have always said that this was my best birthday present I ever received. It came a week late but what the heck. Just a short distance from us was a BOQ for nurses. There was a merry time for all.

Very shortly after the war we were stripped of everything not necessary to run the ship and bunks were placed in every compartment possible. Until I left the ship, December 1, 1945, we were part of the "Magic Carpet" returning military personal from the South Pacific. We carried approximately 15, 000 troops a trip from Pearl to Alameda, CA. and made a round trip every four days.

I had heard that the Sara was to be used as one of the target ships in the A-bomb test. I could have volunteered to be part of those tests, but I just could not bear to see the "Old Lady" sunk. Some years later I read a report that stated that it was not until the second A-bomb that the Sara was sunk. The report further stated that when divers went down to inspect the ship the Sara had a split in her hull from the flight deck to her keel and that was the only major damage. It was nice to know that the Sara was strong until the last.

My Time On Guadalcanal
By Vern Bluhm

To start I should give some background as to why a group of sailors wound up with the Marines on Guadalcanal Island. Here after I will call it the Island or the Canal, though we had some non-repeatable names for it.

When the Marines landed on August 7, 1942, they met rather weak opposition. The first objective was to secure what was to become Henderson Field. The field was captured on the second day, but to secure it became a different matter all together. In back of the field was a half moon set of hills which the Japanese controlled and the field would never be secured until the hills were in the hands of the Marines.

I was a rear seat gunner in a Navy SBD dive bomber aboard the USS Saratoga (CV-3) (we respectfully called her Sara) which was giving the Marines air support. The main problem that developed was that the Marines did not know how to properly control the aircraft. When they would call our aircraft down, they would call the bombs down on themselves or the bombs would land out so far that they were ineffective.

I think in all fairness that I should state a few facts. You have to remember that at this period of the war everyone was learning as they fought. There had been little or no training in jungle warfare. Amphibian warfare was something that the military had little or no training in. Aircraft in support of the ground troops was in its infancy, and for the ground troops to be taught how to control aircraft was mostly nonexistent. These facts are what brought me to the Island.

Our pilots were risking their lives, and were unhappy that they were being so ineffective. I do not think that you could blame them. The Captain of the Sara suggested to Major General Alexander Vandergrift, the commanding general of the 1st Marine Division, that he (Captain of the Sara) send some men over to control the aircraft. I was selected to be part of that team.

When we landed on the Canal we were met with some wariness. One of the first problems that had to be solved was what to do about protection of those who carried the radios. The radios in those days were 90 pound backpacks. It was so bulky that the radioman (radioman=those that carried the radios, not necessarily trained radioman) did not have room to carry a sidearm. The general solved that by assigning two Marine sharpshooters to each radioman. I personally heard the general tell the Marines assigned to us that their one and only job was to stand in between us and a Jap bullet. The reason that aircrew were used instead of trained radiomen was that it was felt that the aircrew would have a better understanding of what the pilots would need to know and could get the proper message to the pilots.

When in a combat zone on the ground, it can be summed up this way. The overwhelming feeling is of being tired, tired in every fiber and bone of your body. You will get so tired that the fear of death is subdued to a great extent. The lack of a good meal and always being dirty soon became accepted as a way of life. The worse fear was when the Japanese navy would shell us every night. You would sit in the bunkers and pray that one of those 16" shells did not land on you. To me and many others this was the worst part of being on the Island. You just sit in the bunker and there was nothing you could do. I knew Marines that had many years in the Corps who cracked during the shelling.

All of us that carried the radios did not go everyday with patrols. We might not go out for a couple days and then there would be times when all of us would be out every day for a week. It mostly depended on whether the Marines were just out probing the Japanese lines or a major push was on. Whether out with a patrol or during a major push and the Marines ran into trouble, we would call in the air support. We usually had fighters and dive bombers over the Island most times in the early part of the campaign, and it depended on the problem as to what type of aircraft was used.

Originally we were supposed to be on the Island just until we secured the field, but the general was so pleased with what we were doing that he kept us until the Island was secured. After the field was secured we controlled the Marine pilots.

Let me end this with this narrative with this statement. The Navy and the Marines were supposed to be deadly enemies. My time with the Marines changed my outlook about them. I returned to my ship with a great of respect for the Marine Corps.

Chapter 5

Korean War Experiences

I was not able to find a Navy Korean veteran who had a story or two about their experiences, so I decided to go ahead and include in this chapter all of the citations of Navy recipients of the Congressional Medal of Honor.

> *During that time the doctors, nurses and corpsman did an outstanding job in caring for the hundreds of Marines and Naval personnel wounded and injured during the Korean war. We would receive several hundred at a time, many directly from a MASH unit, and many directly from the battle field.*
> —William Edwards

Korea War Casualties—169,365 with 54,246 deaths (33,652 KIA), 103,284 wounded, 8,196 MIA and 3,746 POW.

Navy Recipients of the Congressional Medal of Honor during the Korean War
By Donald Johnson

The Korean War had always interested me because my mother's brother, Dean, was an Army veteran of that war. My father was in the Army stationed at Camp Gordon, Georgia during the war. I was born at Camp Gordon. My father's younger brother, Gene, was a Marine and a combat veteran of the war and a Purple Heart recipient. He was wounded twice during three battles of Pork Chop Hill. My father's sister, Marian, married a sailor, Virgil Snyder, who was a Navy veteran of the Korean War and the Vietnam War. I was always reading what I could about the Korean War and I watched every movie made about the war. I watched the movie, Pork Chop Hill, with Gregory Peck over a dozen times over the years. My Uncle Gene was one of my unsung heroes when I was growing up. I know a Navy Corpsman patched him up both times he was wounded.

In my eyes, Navy Corpsmen are unsung heroes. They are out there in battle trying to keep our Marines alive. Five Navy Corpsmen won the Congressional Medal of Honor during the Korean War. Two Navy pilots won the highest honor as well.

The medal was originally awarded to petty officers, seamen, landsmen and marines for gallantry in action and other seamanlike qualities (such as the saving of lives). Officers were not eligible until March 3, 1915, but some awards were made retroactive to earlier campaigns. An Act of Congress on August 7, 1942 established the Medal of Honor as a combat award only. It is the highest award for gallantry that the Army or Navy bestows.

Recipients of the Congressional Medal of Honor (MOH) are those who go above and beyond the call of duty. They care about their fellow shipmates and Marines. The Korean War gave the nation 6 Navy recipients.

Many of those recipients had Navy ships named after them either in memory of or in honor of. I have attached the information about the ships at the end of their MOH citation. The citations are a matter of public domain and can be requested through the Freedom of Information Act. The rest of the information was obtained through research on the Internet or through books that I have in my library. Credit will be given to the author of the information, if known.

Edward C. Benfold, HM3

Edward C. Benfold, Hospital Corpsman Petty Officer Third Class, a U.S. Navy Medical Corpsman, was assigned to the First Marine Division in Korea.

Hospital Corpsman Third Class Edward C. Benfold, USN was born in Staten Island, New York on January 15, 1931, Petty Officer Benfold graduated from Audubon High School in Audubon, New Jersey. Petty Officer Benfold entered the service at Philadelphia, Pennsylvania in 1950. After completion of recruit training in Great Lakes, Illinois, he was selected for "A" school training as a Hospitalman. In July 1951, he was designated as a Medical Field Technician and was ordered to duty with the Fleet Marine Force, Ground, Pacific. He was killed in action while serving with the First Marine Division in Korea.

He received the Congressional Medal of Honor posthumously:

For gallantry and intrepidity at the risk of his life above and beyond the call of duty while serving in operations against enemy aggressor forces. When his company was subjected to heavy artillery and mortar barrages, followed by a determined assault during the hours of darkness by an enemy force estimated at battalion strength, HC3c. Benfold resolutely moved from position to position in the face of intense hostile fire, treating the wounded and lending words of encouragement. Leaving the protection of his sheltered position to treat the wounded when the platoon area in which he was working was attacked from both the front and rear, he moved forward to an exposed ridge line where he observed 2 marines in a large crater. As he approached the 2 men to determine their condition, an enemy soldier threw 2 grenades into the crater while 2 other enemy charged the position. Picking up a grenade in each hand, HC3c Benfold leaped out of the crater and hurled himself against the on-rushing hostile soldiers, pushing the grenades against their chests and killing both the attackers. Mortally wounded while carrying out this heroic act, HC3c. Benfold, by his great personal valor and resolute spirit of self-sacrifice in the face of almost certain death, was directly responsible for saving the lives of his 2 comrades. His exceptional courage reflects the highest credit upon himself and enhances the finest traditions of the U.S. Naval Service. He gallantly gave his life for others.

USS BENFOLD (DDG-65) was named in honor of Hospital Corpsman Third Class Petty Officer Edward C. Benfold and is a multi-mission ship equipped with the modern Aegis combat weapons system, which combines space-age communication, radar and weapons technologies in a single platform for unlimited flexibility.

USS BENFOLD is equipped to carry Standard surface-to-air-missiles and Tomahawk cruise missiles launched from forward and aft vertical launching systems, two radar-controlled Phalanx close-in weapon systems, Harpoon anti-ship missiles, one five-inch gun and electronic warfare systems.

William R. Charette, HM3

William R. Charette, Hospital Corpsman Third Class Petty Officer, a U.S. Navy Medical Corpsman was assigned to a Marine rifle company in Korea on 27 March 1953. He entered the service at Ludington, Michigan.

He received the Congressional Medal of Honor:

For conspicuous gallantry and intrepidity at the risk of his life above and beyond the call of duty in action against enemy aggressor forces during the early morning hours. Participating in a fierce encounter with a cleverly concealed and well-entrenched enemy force occupying positions on a vital and bitterly contested outpost far in advance of the main line of resistance, HC3c. Charette repeatedly and unhesitatingly moved about through a murderous barrage of hostile small-arms and mortar fire to render assistance to his wounded comrades. When an enemy grenade landed within a few feet of a marine he was attending, he immediately threw himself upon the stricken man and absorbed the entire concussion of the deadly missile with his body. Although sustaining painful facial wounds, and undergoing shock from the intensity of the blast which ripped the helmet and medical aid kit from his person, HC3c. Charette resourcefully improvised emergency bandages by tearing off part of his clothing, and gallantly continued to administer medical aid to the wounded in his own unit and to those in adjacent platoon areas as well. Observing a seriously wounded comrade whose armored vest had been torn from his body by the blast from an exploding shell, he selflessly removed his own battle vest and placed it upon the helpless man although fully aware of the added jeopardy to himself. Moving to the side of another casualty who was suffering excruciating pain from a serious leg wound, HC3c. Charette stood upright in the trench line and exposed himself to a deadly hail of enemy fire in order to lend more effective aid to the victim and to alleviate his anguish while being removed to a position of safety. By his indomitable courage and inspiring efforts in behalf of his wounded comrades, HC3c. Charette was directly responsible for saving many lives. His great personal valor reflects the highest credit upon himself and enhances the finest traditions of the U.S. Naval Service.

Richard David Dewert, HM3

Richard David Dewert, Hospital Corpsman Third Class Petty Officer, a U.S. Navy Medical Corpsman, was attached to a Marine infantry company, 1st Marine Division in Korea on 5 April 1951. He entered the service at Taunton, Mass.

He received the Congressional Medal of Honor posthumously:

For conspicuous gallantry and intrepidity at the risk of his life above and beyond the call of duty while serving as a HC, in action against enemy aggressor forces. When a fire team from the point platoon of his company was pinned down by a deadly barrage of hostile automatic weapons fired and suffered many casualties, HC Dewert rushed to the assistance of 1 of the more seriously wounded and, despite a painful leg wound sustained while dragging the stricken marine to safety, steadfastly refused medical treatment for himself and immediately dashed back through the fire swept area to carry a second wounded man out of the line of fire. Undaunted by the mounting hail of devastating enemy fire, he bravely moved forward a third time and received another serious wound in the shoulder after discovering that a wounded marine had already died. Still persistent in his refusal to submit to first aid, he resolutely answered the call of a fourth stricken comrade and, while rendering medical assistance, was himself mortally wounded by a burst of enemy fire. His courageous initiative, great personal valor, and heroic spirit of self-sacrifice in the face of overwhelming odds reflect the highest credit upon HC Dewert and enhance the finest traditions of the U.S. Naval Service. He gallantly gave his life for his country.

USS Dewert (FFG-45) was named in memory of HM3 Richard David Dewert, It is a fast frigate that fulfills a Protection of Shipping (POS) mission as an Anti-Submarine Warfare (ASW) combatant for amphibious expeditionary forces, underway replenishment groups and merchant convoys.

The guided missile frigates (FFG) bring an anti-air warfare (AAW) capability to the frigate mission, but they have some limitations. Designed as cost efficient surface combatants, they lack the multi-mission capability necessary for modern surface combatants faced with multiple, high-technology threats. They also offer limited capacity for growth. Despite this, the FFG 7 class is a robust platform, capable of withstanding considerable damage. This "toughness" was aptly demonstrated when *USS Samuel B. Roberts* struck a mine and *USS Stark* was hit by two *Exocet* cruise missiles. In both cases the ships survived, were repaired and returned to the fleet.

Francis C. Hammond, HM3

Francis C. Hammond, Hospital Corpsman Third Class Petty Officer, a U.S. Navy Medical Corpsman, was attached as a medical corpsman to 1st Marine Division in Korea on 26-27 March 1953. He entered the service at Alexandria, Va.

He received the Congressional Medal of Honor posthumously:

For conspicuous gallantry and intrepidity at the risk of his life above and beyond the call of duty as a HC serving with the 1st Marine Division in action against enemy aggressor forces on the night of 26-27 March 1953. After reaching an intermediate objective during a counterattack against a heavily entrenched and numerically superior hostile force occupying ground on a bitterly contested outpost far in advance of the main line of resistance. HC Hammond's platoon was subjected to a murderous barrage of hostile mortar and artillery fire, followed by a vicious assault by onrushing enemy troops. Resolutely advancing through the veritable curtain of fire to aid his stricken comrades, HC Hammond moved among the stalwart garrison of marines and, although critically wounded he, valiantly continued to administer aid to the other wounded throughout an exhausting 4-hour period. When the unit was ordered to withdraw, he skillfully directed the evacuation of casualties and remained in the fire-swept area to assist the corpsmen of the relieving unit until he was struck by a round of enemy mortar fire and fell, mortally wounded. By his exceptional fortitude, inspiring initiative and self-sacrificing efforts, HC Hammond undoubtedly saved the lives of many marines. His great personal valor in the face of overwhelming odds enhances and sustains the finest traditions of the U.S. Naval Service. He gallantly gave his life for his country.

USS Francis C. HAMMOND (FF-1067) was named in memory of HM3 Francis C. Hammond. It is a fast frigate that was originally designed as a Destroyer Escort, The Knox Class was primarily used as an ASW platform, utilizing the T.A.S (Towed Array Sonar) and the L.A.M.P.S helicopter. It was commissioned on July 25, 1970 and de-commissioned on 2 July 1992.

Thomas Jerome Hudner, Jr., LTJG

Thomas Jerome Hudner, Jr., Lieutenant junior grade (LTJG), a U.S. Navy pilot was assigned to Fighter Squadron 32 that was attached to USS. Leyte and assigned to an area over the Chosin Reservoir in Korea in support of U.S. Marines on December 4, 1950. He entered the service at Fall River, Mass.

In 1948, LT Brown began a tour of duty with VF-32 at Quonset Point, Rhode Island, and was commissioned an Ensign on 15 April of that year. About a year later, Brown met a new pilot named Thomas J. Hudner, a graduate of Phillip's Academy and the US Naval Academy, and also the son of successful Massachusetts business owner.

Brown and Hudner were soon flying together. Despite Lieutenant (Junior Grade) Hudner's higher rank, Navy policy, set flying assignments based on experience, and Ensign Brown had more hours. Hudner was assigned to be Brown's wingman and found Brown a patient and disciplined pilot. But off duty, the two aviators didn't socialize much. In the early Fifties, all the bachelor officers hung out at the Officers' Club. Brown was married, and like most of the married officers, spent his free time with his family. In June 1950, VF-32 was operating from USS Leyte (CV-32) in the Mediterranean on a routine cruise but was soon diverted to the Korean peninsula when the war started. In October 1950, Leyte joined Fast Carrier Task Force 77 in support of the United Nations Forces in Korea. Soon Hudner and Brown were flying F4U-4 Corsair missions from Leyte.

As a pilot of Fighter Squadron 32, Ensign Brown became a section leader and received the Air Medal for daring attacks against the enemy at Wonsan, Chongjin, Songjin, and Sinanju. Leading his section in the face of hostile anti-aircraft fire, he courageously pressed home attacks that inflicted heavy losses on the enemy and provided effective support for friendly ground troops.

On December 4, both pilots were part of a formation of eight Corsairs flying armed reconnaissance patrols near the Chosin Reservoir. "We'd fly around and look for targets of opportunity," Hudner said later. "We didn't have pre-designated targets, but if we saw military equipment, trucks, or troops, we'd destroy them with rockets or our .50-caliber guns. We were high enough to see fairly well ahead, but low enough to see objects and people on the ground. It was very mountainous in that area and we didn't want to go too low. A lot of our planes came back to the ship with small-caliber holes in the wings and fuselage."

Hudner and Brown were at about 1,000 feet when Brown radioed that he was losing oil pressure. "We think it was an oil line that got hit-somebody just got a lucky shot," Hudner said. He crash-landed his plane alongside the wreckage of Ensign Brown's aircraft in a heroic rescue attempt. Despite LTJG Hudner's efforts, Brown perished in the wreckage of his plane.

The next day four Corsairs from Leyte flew over Ensign Brown's plane, and in tribute to a fallen comrade, napalmed the wreckage. The location is Latitude 40 degrees, 36 minutes N; Longitude 127 degrees, 6 minutes East. He was posthumously awarded the Distinguished Flying Cross for his exceptional courage, airmanship, and devotion to duty in the face of great danger.

On April 13, 1951, President Harry Truman presented Hudner with the Medal of Honor in a simple ceremony that included Daisy Brown, Jesse Brown's widow. Despite their different backgrounds, Hudner and Brown had been drawn together by a simple, but powerful brotherhood-a bond graced by a singular and courageous act.

Jesse Brown has been honored as a hero at the Evergreen Aviation Museum in McMinnville, Oregon.

LTJG Hudner received the Congressional Medal of Honor:

For conspicuous gallantry and intrepidity at the risk of his life above and beyond the call of duty as a pilot in Fighter Squadron 32, while attempting to rescue a squadron mate whose plane struck by antiaircraft fire and trailing smoke, was forced down behind enemy lines. Quickly maneuvering to circle the downed pilot and protect him from enemy troops infesting the area, Lt. (J.G.) Hudner risked his life to save the injured flier who was trapped alive in the burning wreckage. Fully aware of the extreme danger in landing on the rough mountainous terrain and the scant hope of escape or survival in subzero temperature, he put his plane down skillfully in a deliberate wheels-up landing in the presence of enemy troops. With his bare hands, he packed the fuselage with snow to keep the flames away from the pilot and struggled to pull him free. Unsuccessful in this, he returned to his crashed aircraft and radioed other airborne planes, requesting that a helicopter be dispatched with an ax and fire extinguisher. He then remained on the spot despite the continuing danger from enemy action and, with the assistance of the rescue pilot, renewed a desperate but unavailing battle against time, cold, and flames. Lt. (J.G.) Hudner's exceptionally valiant action and selfless devotion to a shipmate sustain and enhance the highest traditions of the U.S. Naval Service.

John E. Kilmer, HM3

John E. Kilmer, Hospital Corpsman Third Class Petty Officer, a U.S. Navy medical corpsman was attached to duty with a Marine rifle company in the 1st Marine Division in Korea on 13 August 1952. He entered the service at Houston, Tex.

He received the Congressional Medal of Honor posthumously:

For conspicuous gallantry and intrepidity at the risk of his life above and beyond the call of duty in action against enemy aggressor forces. With his company engaged in defending a vitally important hill position well forward of the main line of resistance during an assault by large concentrations of hostile troops, HC Kilmer repeatedly braved intense enemy mortar, artillery, and sniper fire to move from 1 position to another, administering aid to the wounded and expediting their evacuation. Painfully wounded himself when struck by mortar fragments while moving to the aid of a casualty, he persisted in his efforts and inched his way to the side of the stricken marine through a hail of enemy shells falling around him. Undaunted by the devastating hostile fire, he skillfully administered first aid to his comrade and, as another mounting barrage of enemy fire shattered the immediate area, unhesitatingly shielded the wounded man with his body. Mortally wounded by flying shrapnel while carrying out this heroic action, HC Kilmer, by his great personal valor and gallant spirit of self-sacrifice in saving the life of a comrade, served to inspire all who observed him. His unyielding devotion to duty in the face of heavy odds reflects the highest credit upon himself and enhances the finest traditions of the U.S. Naval Service. He gallantly gave his life for another.

John Kelvin Koelsch, LTJG

John Kelvin Koelsch, Lieutenant junior grade (LTJG), a U.S. Navy pilot assigned to a Navy helicopter rescue unit off the coast of North Korea on July 3, 1951. He entered the service at Los Angeles, Calif.

He received the Congressional Medal of Honor posthumously:

For conspicuous gallantry and intrepidity at the risk of his life above and beyond the call of duty while serving with a Navy helicopter rescue unit. Although darkness was rapidly approaching when information was received that a marine aviator had been shot down and was trapped by the enemy in mountainous terrain deep in hostile territory, Lt. (J.G.) Koelsch voluntarily flew a helicopter to the reported position of the downed airman in an attempt to effect a rescue. With an almost solid overcast concealing everything below the mountain peaks, he descended in his unarmed and vulnerable aircraft without the accompanying fighter escort to an extremely low altitude beneath the cloud level and began a systematic search. Despite the increasingly intense enemy fire, which struck his helicopter on 1 occasion, he persisted in his mission until he succeeded in locating the downed pilot, who was suffering from serious burns on the arms and legs. While the victim was being hoisted into the aircraft, it was struck again by an accurate burst of hostile fire and crashed on the side of the mountain. Quickly extricating his crewmen and the aviator from the wreckage, Lt. (J.G.) Koelsch led them from the vicinity in an effort to escape from hostile troops, evading the enemy forces for 9 days and rendering such medical attention as possible to his severely burned companion until all were captured. Up to the time of his death while still a captive of the enemy, Lt. (J.G.) Koelsch steadfastly refused to aid his captors in any manner and served to inspire his fellow prisoners by his fortitude and consideration for others. His great personal valor and heroic spirit of self-sacrifice throughout sustain and enhance the finest traditions of the U.S. Naval Service.

USS Koelsch (FF-1049) was named in memory of LTJG John Kevin Koelsch. It was commissioned on June 10, 1967 and decommissioned on May 31, 1989.

Chapter 6

Vietnam Experiences

This chapter is one of the longer ones. I have a personal story, a sermon, a story by a heroic sailor and all of the citations for the Navy recipients of the Congressional Medal of Honor included.

Vietnam presumably taught us that the United States could not serve as the world's policeman; it should also have taught us the dangers of trying to be the world's midwife to democracy when the birth is scheduled to take place under conditions of guerrilla war.
—Jeanne Kirkpatrick, 1979

No event in American history is more misunderstood than the Vietnam War. It was misreported then, and it is misremembered now.
—Richard M. Nixon, 1985

Vietnam War Casualties—47,369 KIA, 10,799 non-combat related deaths, 153,303 wounded

LOOKING BACK
By Donald Johnson
Copyright © 2004

This speech was given at one of my many Toastmasters meetings in April 2004.

How many of you have read Tom Brokaw's book, The Greatest Generation?

Did you know that he has a sequel out titled, The Greatest Generation Speaks?

Mr. Toastmaster, fellow Toastmasters and most welcome guests.

My father was a Korean War veteran; however, he had two older brothers who fought in WWII. My uncle Seth was in the Army during WWII and was taken prisoner in Philippines. My uncle Don served on a ship in the Pacific during the Battles of Iwo Jima and Okinawa. My mother's oldest brother, Herb, that spent his entire war effort on a small aircraft carrier in the Pacific which supported the Battle of Okinawa with Combat Air Patrols and close in ground support.

"The Greatest Generation Speaks" did two things for me. It made me think back on the war stories my uncles told me when growing up. It also made me think back on the two wars that I had an active participation in whether I wanted to be there or not.

Tonight I am going to tell you another one of my sea stories.

In 1970 I was stationed aboard the USS Guadalupe. Her hull number was AO-32 and was also known as the Greasy Guadaloop. This was a fleet oiler and the 2nd oldest ship in the Navy at the time. You have to get a picture of what this thing looked like. It was 800 feet long, had two superstructures, one aft and one amidships. The one aft was where the CPOs and officers slept. The enlisted dining facility was located in this same area. The one amidships had the captains cabin, executive officers stateroom along with most of the ships operations spaces such as the radio shack, the combat information center, the ship's bridge and signal bridge.

Between the two superstructures on both port and starboard sides stood stanchions with support arms at the top hanging out seaward. These stanchions were 18" in diameter, stood 30' tall and supported the 200' x 12" hoses that were sent over to refuel ships. Yes, we were a floating gas station. The ship carried 5 million gallons of black oil and 1 million gallons of JP5 aviation fuel.

The ship would send out a schedule for all the other ships in the Gulf of Tonkin to let them know where we would be and what course we would be heading. We operated 10 days on the line (Gulf of Tonkin) and 3 days in port Subic Bay refueling.

On this particular schedule it seems to me that the aircraft carriers were beginning to launch more missions over North Vietnam. We were to refuel all comers who needed fuel. We got to the northern most tip of our operating area and then headed due south. We stayed on this course for over 2 1/2 days. What was significant about this schedule is that I had a replenishment station that I had to man during this schedule. I thought I was going to be able to get relieved sometime during this schedule. Well guess what? None of my good buddies would come down to relieve me. I was a phone talker who kept the crew on the bridge informed of what was happening during the refueling and passed vital information to the bridge. I could not leave my station unless I was properly relieved.

On the first morning of the refueling schedule I decided that I was going to not drink any coffee and to make sure that I made my nature calls before going to my refueling station. I was also experimenting with speed at the time. I have told people over and over that I didn't do that stuff on board the ship. Well I have lied to people all of these years. My buddies knew I was experimenting just like they were.

When we first got started refueling ships, it was 8 a.m. about 50 miles off Haiphong Harbor in North Vietnam. We were heading due south and had to refuel a cruiser, the St. Paul and a destroyer whose name I can't recall. The oiler sets a course and speed and maintains them. The ships needing refueling come along side and once they are in place going the same speed and course as us, then we send over shot lines, a shot gun with a projectile with a long piece of heavy string attached. That starts the heavy rope and then the wire cable. Once the wire cable is over, it is secured to a locking device and then the huge hoses with a refueling probe are sent over to be inserted into a fitting to begin the refueling process.

My duty was to inform the bridge as to when the shot line, the rope and wire cable had been sent over and secured. I then passed the word up when the hoses began going over. I also passed the word up to how many gallons had been pumped every 30 minutes or so and any other word that the refueling officers and chief petty officers wanted passed up to the captain.

This process went on for over 60 hours. We refueled 36 ships which included 8 aircraft carriers which took 4 hours each to refuel. We refueled two at a time. We also refueled 4 cruisers, 1 battleship (NJ), 10 destroyers, 8 fast frigates, 4 Australian destroyers and 2 Coast Guard cutters.

I stayed up for 60 hours and not all at my refueling station. We got breaks in between refueling jobs to get something to eat and if we could, some sleep. I had tried numerous times to get a relief.

The only thing that kept me going during that 60 hours was the speed that I took. When the refueling evolutions were done after 60 hours, I was so drained that I fell a sleep in my bunk and slept for over 12 hours.

I won't tell you what I said to my so-called buddies after I woke. I also had a meeting with my chief petty officer to tell him about my displeasure in the incident and how by having me on station that long could have caused a serious safety hazard.

I was weaned off the speed shortly after returning to Long Beach. Since those days I have been strongly opposed the use of illegal drugs and what they do to people and what they could have done to me until I was brought to my senses by a friend.

Today as I continue to read the letters in The Greatest Generation Speaks, I will continue to look back on my Navy days and the two wars that I proudly say I served.

A Ladder to Heaven
By Donald Johnson
©2005 by Donald Johnson

Note: I have included one of my earliest sermons. This is a sermon on Jacob's ladder. You sailors all know what a Jacob's ladder is. I look back at my early Navy days and I know that God was there the entire time. There is some humor in this sermon so do not worry too much about becoming bored.

Let us go to the Lord in prayer.

"Gracious God—bless now the words of my lips and the meditations of our hearts. Breathe your Spirit into us and grant that we may hear and in hearing be led in the way you want us to go. Amen.

How many of you know what Jacob's ladder is? Do you really? This morning I am going to tell you about three types of Jacob's ladders. Let me know later which one you identify with. I identify with all three.

The first Jacob's ladder that I am going to tell you about appeared in the story of Jacob's ladder in the Book of Genesis.

Here we have a man, Jacob, who deceived his father and brother so that he could become the blessed son, a blessing that was supposed to go to his older brother, Esau.

Before his trouble began, Jacob was not really a religious man. This guy was into doing household chores such as cooking gourmet meals. He was a mama's boy. I have nothing against mama's boys, because you see, I was a mama's boy for the first 16 years of my life.

Rebekah loved Jacob so much that she helped him deceive his father and brother, but afterwards she felt guilty about what she had done. She also knew that Esau was going to harm Jacob, so she warns him to get out of Dodge before Esau kills him.

Jacob takes off to escape his brother's wrath. After being on the run for a while, Jacob had time to think. He was probably wondering how he got himself into this situation. All of a sudden, he was feeling down and lost and frustrated with life.

You cannot be on the run too awfully long before you start to become tired. Jacob was tired, dog tired and wanted to lie down and sleep. He chose a rock of all things to use as a pillow. How about you? Would you use a rock as a pillow? Not me. I am not the outdoors type. Ask Barbara.............. My idea of camping is an RV with all the amenities of home. A thick mattress, Dish TV so I can get my Fox News, a microwave for my popcorn, running water for cooking and a nice hot shower in the morning, you know what I am talking about? I guess that is some of the mama's boy coming out in me again.

I, myself, have suffered from dog tiredness many times especially while out at sea. During combat operations, many sailors do not get much sleep. I can remember one time while stationed aboard an old nasty navy oiler when we began our trip from the Gulf of Tonkin or Yankee Station off North Vietnam and headed southeast to begin refueling operations of 27 ships that I did not sleep for almost 60 hours.

When I was finally dismissed from my at sea refueling station upon completing the refueling of the 27th ship, I went down to hop up into my bunk. This bunk consisted of an aluminum frame, a canvas backing and a 2" thick mattress. Bunks were stacked four high on this ship. Guess where mine was? I used the bottom three bunks as a ladder to climb into the top bunk. Once in my bunk, I began to look at it for once as a place of comfort. I used to hate that bunk because it was up high and it was too short for my long body. I closed my eyes and promptly fell asleep. I could not be woken for the next 12 hours. I now considered my bunk as a place that I could go to get comfort when I was tired. I was like Jacob in a way. He resigned himself to lying on the ground with a rock for his pillow. I resigned myself to sleeping on a 2" mattress with a canvas-backed frame that was situated about 6-7 feet up from the steel deck. I guess I can say I was a little closer to heaven than Jacob.

After Jacob fell asleep, he dreamed of a stairway to heaven with angels ascending and descending and God was at the top of the staircase. He awoke from that dream a believer in God but also scared and still somewhat reluctant. In Genesis 28 verse 17, it says "He was afraid and said, 'How awesome is this place! This is none other than the house of God; this is the gate of heaven.'" My interpretation of this story is a simple one. God was trying to tell Jacob, "Hey, dude, I am here. I am here to comfort you during times of trouble and these angels will be ministering to your needs as well as the needs of your loved ones." The angels descending were bringing their orders down from God while the ones ascending had completed their mission and were heading back up for new orders.

The ministering of angels is seen throughout the Bible. This morning the two scriptures had two words in common—Descending and Ascending.

Now talking about descending and ascending, how many of you know that in this world there is a real physical thing called a Jacob's ladder? This is the second Jacob's ladder that I am going to speak about. The Navy has a Jacob's ladder that is a ladder made of rope (line) or steel cable and the rungs are about 15" wide and if you attach wood or strips of steel or aluminum to the rungs, it becomes easier to climb up and down. A Jacob's ladder is used most often for sailors to descend from and ascend to the main deck of ships and a rescue boat called a motor whaleboat. They normally hang from a boom or an arm and are swung out over the water and then lowered. A Jacob's ladder is then lowered from the arm so that sailors can descend with their orders and ascend after completing their mission.

The Navy Jacob's ladder has been used extensively in many different operations. After the fall of South Vietnam to the North, many Vietnamese escaped the wrath of the North by leaving in boats, all types of boats, some seaworthy and some not. During Operation Refugee, if Navy ships came upon Vietnamese refugee boats, they would send a rescue boat over to see what they needed. If the boat was seaworthy, the boat people would be given instructions on how to get to the nearest and safest land, primarily the Philippines, Singapore or Thailand, and given enough fuel, food and water to get them there.

Sometimes the boats were not seaworthy with engines that were no longer running, they were out of food and water and many of the boat occupants had health problems. That was when the commanding officer made a decision to take them all onboard and take care of them until the ship's next port of call.

After being at sea for weeks and sometimes months, a U.S. Navy ship was a heavenly thing to see. They knew that American sailors would take care of them in one way or another. That Jacob's ladder that they had to climb was their bridge from hell to heaven. All they were looking for was a place they could live in freedom and a place they could worship without being harmed. They would find that in the U.S. if they made it that far. The Navy gave them food and water, medical care and a place to shower and a place to sleep. Do you think they cared if they slept in a bunk with a 4" mattress? I do not think so. That Navy Jacob's ladder took them to a place of comfort, a place they thought was heaven.

I see some of you mathematicians out there thinking. Yes, the mattresses started out as a 2" mattress and now it is 4" and yes, they are getting thicker and if I was going to tell you more sea stories, by the time my sermon is over, they should be a foot thick. I know one thing that if I ever buy an RV it will have a 12" mattress for me lie down on at night. However, I am not going to tell you any more sea stories.

I am going to take you back to the Gospel reading.

In verse 51, Jesus said, I tell you the truth, you shall see heaven open and the angels of God ascending and descending on the Son of Man.

Is that not almost word for word that was in the Genesis scripture? What does the Gospel passage tell me? This scripture takes me to the third Jacob's ladder. It tells me that Jesus Christ is today's spiritual Jacob's ladder. You cannot get to heaven except through Jesus Christ. God sent Jesus to us to bridge that gap between us sinners and him. He gave his only Son so that...we would have a stairway to heaven.

And that stairway once again is Jesus Christ and He is the only way.

If you continue to read about Jacob, you will see that he became a changed man because of his belief and faith in God. God promised Jacob many things and Jacob said that if God did those things he would do certain things in return, and one of those things was to tithe 10% of everything. Jacob made a vow to God and he kept it. Because of his actions, he began to change, change for the better. Jacob was still skeptical at the very beginning, but as God began to fulfill his promises, Jacob began to fulfill his.

Many people in this world have multiple problems and have no idea how to take care of those problems. All they have to do is make one choice in their life and that is to accept Jesus Christ as their Lord and Savior and stay true to that vow, ask God for help and they will see change, positive change become a part of their life or lives. It takes a long time sometimes for your life to fall into place.

As in my case, 7 years ago I gave my life to Jesus Christ once again to let Him run my daily affairs. Since that time, He has guided me through some very troubled times, but life is getting better and I have definitely changed. Sometimes I still struggle with Him. But as we all know, we cannot win. When I finally reach that conclusion, I just give up and say, "Whatever Lord! I'm yours."

John Newton the slave-trader turned hymn-writer after his conversion said: "Though I am not what I ought to be, nor what I wish to be, nor yet what I hope to be, I can truly say I am not what I once was: a slave to sin and Satan."

Salvation from sin, transformation to a new person, and reconciliation to God are made possible in Christ (John 1:51). Jesus Christ is the ladder or stairway between heaven and earth and between God and man.

It has been my prayer since becoming a born-again Christian for all people to turn away from sin, turn to Him, and turn their lives around just as Jacob did?

If you are doing that, then you are definitely climbing Jacob's ladder. I do challenge you to share your Christian beliefs with someone who is having troubles. If you do and they listen, then you have started that person on their climb up Jacob's ladder. So go out and Make A Difference In Your World and be a witness to Jesus Christ.

Thanks be to God who gives us the victory through our Lord Jesus Christ. Amen

The Forrestal Fire
by Don Cook

I worked on the flight deck during the night check crew attached to Fighter Squadron eleven (VF-11). As a plane captain, I was in charge of my aircraft mechanically and was inseparable during its time on deck. My plane was a McDonald Douglas F4-B Phantom two seat fighter. The daily routine off the coast of North Viet Nam was a twenty four hour a day operation with each combat sortie lasting between forty five minutes to one and a half hours. I think it was a night or two before the fire, I remember a member of the VF-11 ordinance crew was arming missiles and bombs as the aircraft was rolling up to the catapult. I don't remember the crewmen's name but, as he was moving about under the moving aircraft, he fell and the F4 Phantom rolled over his foot then, pinning him, rolled over his shoulder. The night before the fire Tim Michelfelder and I went to visit our injured shipmate in sick bay. The part of his arm we could see was black and we heard from medic's in sick bay that he was going to loose his arm. The flight deck, at night in combat, was not for the faint hearted.

My flight deck duties ended at 0800 hours. I hit the sack at about 1000 hours. VF-11 berthing space was located on the 03 level (just below the flight deck) and aft of the arresting gear engines. It was an area that was difficult to get a good night sleep. Fifty thousand pound aircraft landing within a few feet overhead, just forward the arresting gear engines howling as they pay out one and a half inch diameter arresting gear cable to bring the aircraft to a halt in less that two hundred feet. The ship's four, twenty two foot, five blade propellers were directly below at about seven decks.

At 10:52 I awoke to the 1MC (a loud speaker public address system) blaring, "Fire, Fire, Fire on the flight deck aft". Just as I was getting up the first one thousand pound bomb detonated on the port side forward of our compartment. (Now, thirty three years later, if I don't sleep well I'll suddenly awake to that sound of a grossly over amplified BANG in a pitch black compartment and find myself on the floor) My friend Joe Kosik, said that he thought a plane had crashed on the flight deck and then disappeared in the smoke. I never saw Joe again. The compartment quickly filled with thick black smoke. Overhead light fixtures came crashing down and a locker fell on my foot causing an ankle to become dislocated. Fire balls boiled slowly along the overhead in the port 03 passageway imparting an unearthly glow in the smoke and silhouetting crew-men moving about in the compartment.

Most of the VF-11 night crew were congregating on the port side due to the debris laying about. I was on the starboard side of the compartment. I wanted to get over to my friends but was blocked by debris. Larry Huxoll came by with a flashlight and quickly decided to exit the compartment. When confronted by a fire your natural tendency is to move away from it. Huxoll and I went down a starboard hatch, down the ladder three decks to the hanger deck. (the main deck) The hatch to enter lower levels of the ship were dogged. We then entered the huge expanse of the number three hanger bay. It was, like everywhere else we had tried, filled with smoke and totally closed. (condition Zebra).
We knew if we tried to find our way in the black smoke filled hanger we would not get out. Also there was about a foot or two of water in the hanger bay which made us think the ship was going down. We then heard another bomb cook off, the ship shuttered. We knew then that we had little time left to escape. We climbed the ladder back up three decks to the 03. The 03 passageway runs nearly the full length of the ship with few dogged hatches but at each frame an oval cut out that is about a foot short of opening to the deck. These oval open-ings are affectionately called "knee Knockers" by the crew. Huxoll and I stood outside the compartment to consider going back in. We didn't hear any voices or noise except the activity above on the flight deck. We thought we were the last of the crew still back in the aft portion of the 03. Quickly we moved for-ward to what we thought was suicide because we were moving toward the fire but we were out of options. At some point we came upon an OBA locker (Oxygen Breathing Apparatus) but there wasn't any OBA's in the locker. I remember thinking to myself, I wonder what my parents are going to think when they find my burnt body back in the aft passageway. We would walk, as the deck was getting hotter and hotter, until our leg's hit a "Knee Knocker" with a thud again and again until we came to a frame with light and fresh air, probably about amidships. We were quickly escorted away to a compartment and given blankets because we were covered in soot and looked as if we were badly burnt. First aid was applied to our hammered legs and an ace bandage for the ankle. The first thing we asked for was a cigarette. You would think after breathing that much smoke the last thing you would be interested in was more. We were asked if we had seen any other crew back aft. We responded that we thought we were the last out.

At some point, after we were at this compartment, a thousand pound bomb went off over our berthing compartment killing everyone in the compartment.

From that point we were brought to the number one hanger bay starboard elevator and we were helped with donning life jackets because most crew thought we may go down. As we sat next to the elevator door the elevator came down to the hanger bay with a completely nude crew men standing with his arms stretched out like he had been nailed to a cross. An IV bottle with a line that snaked into his arm and large sheets of broiled skin hung off his body like sails. Soon we were given clothing and headed up to the flight deck. My general quarters station was my aircraft but it had been destroyed. Huxoll and I volunteered to man a fire hose but we were not allowed because we didn't have flight deck boots on. We had been given shower shoes in the rush. As I sat on a tow bar waiting for someone to bring up a pair of shoes I noticed an odd piece of material lying next to the bar. as I picked it up I froze, it was a piece of tissue, human hair on one side, and what looked like hamburger on the other. Within an hour or two the fire on the flight deck was under control.

Sick bay, on the Forrestal, was located on the deck just below the hanger (2nd deck) and between the aft and forward galleys. Due to the fire there was not access to sick bay via the aft hatch. All injured crew members were rushed down the ladders to the forward galley then thought the galley to the sick bay. The walls and ladder were blasted everywhere with blood. We didn't eat in the galley for days afterward due to the reminder leading down to the galley of just what our shipmates had endured. One of the most persistent memories I have are of the Vigilante recon aircraft being thrown overboard on the port angle to my left and the nude sailor on my right. Every time I see that footage (the aircraft being tossed overboard) in "Situation Critical" I remember the smell of blood and smoke.

A few days after we were back in Subic Bay K.B. Deering and I went to a, I don't know what to call it, ship's company get together at a large Quonset hut at Subic Naval Station. What a brawl, We knew how to blow steam off in those days. Even the base marines left us alone that night.

On the trip back to the U.S. the ship labored through high winds and heavy sea's south of the Cape of Good Hope South Africa.

With the pitching and rolling of the ship, large cracks caused by the bombs began to expand. A watch was formed call a "crack watch". We would strike a line with white chalk and date it to determine the rate of expansion of the crack. During one of those watches, I think midnight to 0400 hundred hours, (the Dog Watch) I walked back aft on the 03. A string of sixty watt light bulbs had been temporally strung to illuminate the ghostly passageway. I marked the cracks and dated them when I noticed a spot of tile left unburned on the deck. It was a spot roughly in the shape of a cross and it was where I had found my friend. My father died of a heart attack when the ship was near Puerto Rico. I flew off the ship to attend my dad's funeral having not seen the welcome home at Mayport, Florida.

Navy Recipients of the Congressional Medal of Honor during the Vietnam War Era
By Donald Johnson

The Vietnam War is one that I am very familiar with. I am a Vietnam veteran who never saw combat. I was stationed aboard a Navy oiler serving in a non-combat support role of refueling other ships serving in combat support operations.

It was also a controversial war that nearly ripped our nation apart. Many loved ones were killed. A school mate of mine who became a Marine shortly after he graduated was killed while I was in boot camp. My wife lost a cousin.

I can remember going home on boot camp leave in September 1970 to arrive just days before my Grandpa Johnson died and I wore my uniform for his funeral. He was a World War I Army veteran and lived in a small town in southeastern Kansas. Patriotism was still high in small town America. I don't believe that patriotism really left small town America. Or at least it didn't in that town.

I did wear my uniform to two high school graduations in the Wichita area while on boot camp leave. The brother of my dead school mate came up to me at one of them and screamed and yelled at me and spit at me and tried to punch me. I decided to leave before a bad situation turned into a worse situation.

I then left to Radioman school in Bainbridge, Maryland. One of my instructors Radioman First Class Turner was a combat veteran of the war. He backpacked radios for the Marines. The Marines were losing their radiomen so fast that they had to turn to the Navy for radiomen. In 1971, I swapped ships with a Navy radioman who had been a backpacker with the Marines and was also a Purple Heart recipient. He wanted to head back overseas. I was in the process of getting married.

So once again the Marines had their few good men. This time it was not only the Navy Corpsmen but also Navy radiomen.

No Navy radiomen were awarded the Congressional Medal of Honor, but four Navy Corpsmen did. Additionally, three Navy pilots, three Navy SEALS, one Navy SEABEE, three river boat assault squadron sailors, one Navy chaplain and the commanding officer of an electronic surveillance ship that was attacked by the Israelis during the Six Day War in 1967 received the nation's highest honor. All are unsung heroes.

Recipients of the Congressional Medal of Honor (MOH) are those who go above and beyond the call of duty. They care about their fellow shipmates and Marines. The Vietnam War Era gave the nation 15 Navy recipients from the Vietnam War and 1 from the Middle East during the Israeli/Arab Six Day War in 1967.

Many of those recipients had Navy ships named after them either in memory of or in honor of. I have attached the information about the ships at the end of their MOH citation. The citations are a matter of public domain and can be requested through the Freedom of Information Act. The rest of the information was obtained through research on the Internet or through books that I have in my library. Credit will be given to the author of the information, if known.

Now sit back and read about some of our Vietnam Navy heroes.

Donald E. Ballard, HM2

Donald E. Ballard was a U.S. Navy Hospital Corpsman Second Class assigned to Company M, 3rd Battalion, 4th Marines, 3rd Marine Division, Quang Tri Province, Republic of Vietnam on 16 May 1968.

He received the Congressional Medal of Honor:

For conspicuous gallantry and intrepidity at the risk of his life above and beyond the call of duty on 16 May 1968 while serving as a Corpsman with Company M, 3d Battalion, 4th Marines, 3d Marine Division in connection with operations against enemy aggressor forces in the Republic of Vietnam. During the afternoon hours, Company M was moving to join the remainder of the 3d Battalion in Quang Tri Province. After treating and evacuating two heat casualties, Petty Officer Ballard was returning to his platoon from the evacuation landing zone when the company was ambushed by a North Vietnamese Army unit employing automatic weapons and mortars, and sustained numerous casualties. Observing a wounded Marine, Petty Officer Ballard unhesitatingly moved across the fire-swept terrain to the injured man and swiftly rendered medical assistance to his comrade. Petty Officer Ballard then directed four Marines to carry the casualty to a position of relative safety. As the four men prepared to move the wounded Marine, an enemy soldier suddenly left his concealed position and, after hurling a hand grenade which landed near the casualty, commenced firing upon the small group of men. Instantly shouting a warning to the Marines, Petty Officer Ballard fearlessly threw himself upon the lethal explosive device to protect his comrades from the deadly blast. When the grenade failed to detonate, he calmly arose from his dangerous position and resolutely continued his determined efforts in treating other Marine casualties. Petty Officer Ballard's heroic actions and selfless concern for the welfare of his companions served to inspire all who observed him and prevented possible injury or death to his fellow Marines. His courage, daring initiative, and unwavering devotion to duty in the face of extreme personal danger, sustain and enhance the finest traditions of the United States Naval Service.

Vincent R. Capodanno, LT

Lieutenant Vincent R. Capodanno was a U.S. Navy Chaplain assigned to the 3rd Battalion, 5th Marines, 1st Marine Division (Rein), FMF, Quang Tin Province, Republic of Vietnam on 4 September 1967.

He received the Congressional Medal of Honor posthumously:

For conspicuous gallantry and intrepidity at the risk of his life above and beyond the call of duty as Chaplain of the 3d Battalion, 5th Marines, 1st Marine Division (Reinforced), Fleet Marine Force, in connection with operations against enemy forces in Quang Tin Province, Republic of Vietnam on 4 September 1967. In response to reports that the 2d Platoon of M Company was in danger of being overrun by a massed enemy assaulting force, Lieutenant Capodanno left the relative safety of the Company Command Post and ran through an open area raked with fire, directly to the beleaguered platoon. Disregarding the intense enemy small-arms, automatic-weapons, and mortar fire, he moved about the battlefield administering last rites to the dying and giving medical aid to the wounded. When an exploding mortar round inflicted painful multiple wounds to his arms and legs, and severed a portion of his right hand, he steadfastly refused all medical aid. Instead, he directed the corpsmen to help their wounded comrades and, with calm vigor, continued to move about the battlefield as he provided encouragement by voice and example to the valiant Marines. Upon encountering a wounded corpsman in the direct line of fire of an enemy machine gun positioned approximately fifteen yards away, Lieutenant Capodanno rushed forward in a daring attempt to aid and assist the mortally wounded corpsman. At that instant, only inches from his goal, he was struck down by a burst of machine gun fire. By his heroic conduct on the battlefield, and his inspiring example, Lieutenant Capodanno upheld the finest traditions of the United States Naval Service. He gallantly gave his life in the cause of freedom.

USS Capodanno (FF-1093) was named in memory of Lieutenant Capodanno. The ships was commissioned on November 17, 1973 and decommissioned on July 30, 1993.

Wayne Maurice Caron, HM3

Wayne Maurice Caron was a U.S. Navy Hospital Corpsman Third Class assigned to Headquarters and Service Company, 3rd Battalion, 7th Marines, 1st Marine Division (Rein), FMF, Quang Nam Province, Republic of Vietnam on 28 July 1968.

He received the Congressional Medal of Honor posthumously:

For conspicuous gallantry and intrepidity at the risk of his life above and beyond the call of duty on 28 July 1968 while serving as Platoon Corpsman with Company K, 3d Battalion, 7th Marines, 1st Marine Division during combat operations against enemy forces in the Republic of Vietnam. While on a sweep through an open rice field in Quang Nam Province, Petty Officer Caron's unit started receiving enemy small-arms fire. Upon seeing two Marine casualties fall, he immediately ran forward to render first aid, but found that they were dead. At this time, the platoon was taken under intense small-arms and automatic-weapons fire, sustaining additional casualties. As he moved to the aid of his wounded comrades, Petty Officer Caron was hit in the arm by enemy fire. Although knocked to the ground, he regained his feet and continued to the injured Marines. He rendered medical assistance to the first Marine he reached, who was grievously wounded, and undoubtedly was instrumental in saving the man's life. Petty Officer Caron then ran toward the second wounded Marine, but was again hit by enemy fire, this time in the leg. Nonetheless, he crawled the remaining distance and provided medical aid for this severely wounded man. Petty Officer Caron started to make his way to yet another injured comrade, when he was again struck by enemy small-arms fire. Courageously and with unbelievable determination, Petty Officer Caron continued his attempt to reach the third Marine until he himself was killed by an enemy rocket round. His inspiring valor, steadfast determination, and selfless dedication in the face of extreme danger, sustain and enhance the finest traditions of the United States Naval Service.

USS Caron (DD-970) was named in memory of HM3 Caron. USS Caron was the eighth SPRUANCE—class destroyer and the first ship in the Navy named after Hospital Corpsman Third Class Wayne Maurice Caron.

During USS Caron's more than 20 years of service, she had been involved in every conflict that the US had been involved in since her commissioning. Caron has been in Grenada, the Gulf of Sidra, the Black Sea and the Gulf War.

USS Caron was last homeported in Norfolk, Va. On December 4, 2002, she was "accidentally" sunk as a target during explosive tests off Puerto Rico as Caron was believed to survive the tests and scheduled to be sunk as a target in 2003. Secondary explosions during the test finally caused her to sink. USS Caron was the first VLS-equipped ship ever used as target during a SINKEX.

Michael J. Estocin, LCDR

Captain (then LCDR) **Michael J. Estocin**, a U.S. Navy pilot was assigned to Attack Squadron 192, USS Ticonderoga (CVA-14) near Haiphong, North Vietnam on 20 and 26 April 1967.

Captain Estocin received the Congressional Medal of Honor posthumously:

For conspicuous gallantry and intrepidity at the risk of his life above and beyond the call of duty on 20 and 26 April 1967 as a pilot in Attack Squadron One Hundred Ninety-Two, embarked in USS Ticonderoga (CVA 14). Leading a three-plane group of aircraft in support of a coordinated strike against two thermal power plants in Haiphong, North Vietnam, on 20 April 1967, Captain (then Lieutenant Commander) Estocin provided continuous warnings to the strike group leaders of the surface-to-air missile (SAM) threats, and personally neutralized three SAM sites. Although his aircraft was severely damaged by an exploding missile, he reentered the target area and relentlessly prosecuted a Shrike attack in the face of intense antiaircraft fire. With less than five minutes of fuel remaining he departed the target area and commenced in-flight refueling which continued for over one hundred miles. Three miles aft of Ticonderoga, and without enough fuel for a second approach, he disengaged from the tanker and executed a precise approach to a fiery arrested landing. On 26 April 1967, in the support of a coordinated strike against the vital fuel facilities in Haiphong, he led an attack on a threatening SAM site, during which his aircraft was seriously damaged by an exploding SAM; nevertheless, he regained control of his burning aircraft and courageously launched his Shrike missiles before departing the area. By his inspiring courage and unswerving devotion to duty in the face of grave personal danger, Captain Estocin upheld the highest traditions of the United States Naval Service.

USS Estocin (FFG-15), ninth ship of the Oliver Hazard Perry class of guided-missile frigates, was named in memory of Captain John Michael Estocin (1931-1967). Ordered from Bath Iron Works on 27 February 1976 as part of the FY76 program, Estocin was laid down 2 April 1979, launched 3 November 1979, and commissioned 10 January 1981. Decommissioned and stricken 4 April 2003, Estocin was on the same day transferred to Turkey.

Robert R. Ingram, HM3

Robert R. Ingram was a U.S. Navy Hospital Corpsman Third Class assigned to Company C, 1st Battalion, 7th Marines, Quang Ngai Province, Republic of Vietnam on 28 March 1966.

He received the Congressional Medal of Honor:

For conspicuous gallantry and intrepidity at the risk of his life above and beyond the call of duty while serving as Corpsman with Company C, First Battalion, Seventh Marines against elements of a North Vietnam Aggressor (NVA) battalion in Quang Ngai Province Republic of Vietnam on 28 March 1966. Petty Officer Ingram accompanied the point platoon as it aggressively dispatched an outpost of an NVA battalion. The momentum of the attack rolled off a ridge line down a tree covered slope to a small paddy and a village beyond. Suddenly, the village tree line exploded with an intense hail of automatic rifle fire from approximately 100 North Vietnamese regulars. In mere moments, the platoon ranks were decimated. Oblivious to the danger, Petty Officer Ingram crawled across the bullet spattered terrain to reach a downed Marine. As he administered aid, a bullet went through the palm of his hand. Calls for "CORPSMAN" echoed across the ridge. Bleeding, he edged across the fire swept landscape, collecting ammunition from the dead and administering aid to the wounded. Receiving two more wounds before realizing the third wound was life-threatening, he looked for a way off the face of the ridge, but again he heard the call for corpsman and again, he resolutely answered. Though severely wounded three times, he rendered aid to those incapable until he finally reached the right flank of the platoon. While dressing the head wound of another corpsman, he sustained his fourth bullet wound. From sixteen hundred hours until just prior to sunset, Petty Officer Ingram pushed, pulled, cajoled, and doctored his Marines. Enduring the pain from his many wounds and disregarding the probability of his demise, Petty Officer Ingram's intrepid actions saved many lives that day. By his indomitable fighting spirit, daring initiative, and unfaltering dedications to duty, Petty Officer Ingram reflected great credit upon himself and upheld the highest traditions of the United States Naval Service.

[Note: The medal was presented to Retired Petty Officer Ingram at the White House on 10 July 1998.]

Thomas G. Kelley, LCDR

Lieutenant Commander Thomas G. Kelley, a U.S. Navy assault boat commander, was assigned to River Assault Division 152, Ong Muong Canal, Kien Hoa province, Republic of Vietnam on 15 June 1969.

He received the Congressional Medal of Honor:

For conspicuous gallantry and intrepidity at the risk of his life above and beyond the call of duty on the afternoon of 15 June 1969 while serving as Commander River Assault Division 152 during combat operations against enemy aggressor forces in the Republic of Vietnam. Lieutenant Kelley was in charge of a column of eight river assault craft which were extracting one company of United States Army infantry troops on the east bank of the Ong Muong Canal in Kien Hoa Province, when one of the armored troop carriers reported a mechanical failure of a loading ramp. At approximately the same time, Viet Cong forces opened fire from the opposite bank of the canal. After issuing orders for the crippled troop carrier to raise its ramp manually, and for the remaining boats to form a protective cordon around the disabled craft, Lieutenant Kelley, realizing the extreme danger to his column and its inability to clear the ambush site until the crippled unit was repaired, boldly maneuvered the monitor in which he was embarked to the exposed side of the protective cordon in direct line with the enemy's fire, and ordered the monitor to commence firing. Suddenly, an enemy rocket scored a direct hit on the coxswain's flat, the shell penetrating the thick armor plate, and the explosion spraying shrapnel in all directions. Sustaining serious head wounds from the blast, which hurled him to the deck of the monitor, Lieutenant Kelley disregarded his severe injuries and attempted to continue directing the other boats. Although unable to move from the deck or to speak clearly into the radio, he succeeded in relaying his commands through one of his men until the enemy attack was silenced and the boats were able to move to an area of safety. Lieutenant Kelley's brilliant leadership, bold initiative, and resolute determination served to inspire his men and provided the impetus needed to carry out the mission after he was medically evacuated by helicopter. His extraordinary courage under fire, and his selfless devotion to duty sustain and enhance the finest traditions of the United States Naval Service.

Joseph R. Kerrey, LTJG

Lieutenant, Junior Grade, Joseph R. Kerrey, a U.S. Navy SEAL, was assigned to a Sea, Air, and Land (SEAL) Team near Nha Trang Bay, Republic of Vietnam on 14 March 1969.

He received the Congressional Medal of Honor:

For conspicuous gallantry and intrepidity at the risk of his life above and beyond the call of duty on 14 March 1969 while serving as a SEAL Team Leader during action against enemy aggressor (Viet Cong) forces in the Republic of Vietnam. Acting in response to reliable intelligence, Lieutenant (jg) Kerrey lead his SEAL Team on a mission to capture important members of the enemy's area political cadre known to be located on an island in the bay of Nha Trang. In order to surprise the enemy, he and his team scaled a 350-foot sheer cliff to place themselves above the ledge on which the enemy was located. Splitting his team in two elements and coordinating both, Lieutenant (jg) Kerrey led his men in the treacherous downward descent to the enemy's camp. Just as they neared the end of their descent, intense enemy fire was directed at them, and Lieutenant (jg) Kerrey received massive injuries from a grenade which exploded at his feet and threw him backward onto the jagged rocks. Although bleeding profusely and suffering great pain, he displayed outstanding courage and presence of mind in immediately directing his element's fire into the heart of the enemy camp. Utilizing his radioman, Lieutenant (jg) Kerrey called in the second element's fire support which caught the confused Viet Cong in a devastating cross fire. After successfully suppressing the enemy's fire, and although immobilized by his multiple wounds, he continued to maintain calm, superlative control as he ordered his team to secure and defend an extraction site. Lieutenant (jg) Kerrey resolutely directed his men, despite his near-unconscious state, until he was eventually evacuated by helicopter. The havoc brought to the enemy by this very successful mission cannot be overestimated. The enemy who were captured provided critical intelligence to the allied effort. Lieutenant (jg) Kerrey's courageous and inspiring leadership, valiant fighting spirit, and tenacious devotion to duty in the face of almost overwhelming opposition, sustain and enhance the finest traditions of the United States Naval Service.

Note: Joseph R. (Bob) Kerrey later ran for and was elected as a Senator from the Great State of Nebraska.

Clyde Everett Lassen, LT

Lieutenant Clyde Everett Lassen was a U.S. Navy helicopter pilot assigned to Helicopter Support Squadron 7, Detachment 104, embarked in U.S.S. Preble (DLG-15), Republic of Vietnam on 19 June 1968.

Clyde Everett Lassen, a native of Fort Myers, Florida, earned the Congressional Medal of Honor for his courageous rescue of two downed aviators while commander of a search and rescue helicopter in Vietnam.

On June 19, 1968, Lassen, then a 27 year old Lieutenant flying a UH-2 Seasprite, embarked on a mission to recover two downed naval aviators whose plane had been shot down deep in North Vietnamese territory. Upon reaching the hilly terrain where the aviators were hiding, LT Lassen made several attempts to recover the aviators, but dense tree cover, enemy weapons fire and intermittent illumination frustrated his efforts. Determined to complete his mission, LT Lassen turned on the landing lights of the helicopter, despite the danger of revealing his position to the enemy. After the pilots made their way to the helicopter and with his damaged helicopter dangerously low on fuel, LT Lassen evaded further antiaircraft fire before landing safely at sea onboard a guided missile destroyer-with only five minutes of fuel left in the helicopter's fuel lines.

The account of the rescue was logged as a successful, routine search and rescue mission. But at the home base for Helicopter Combat Squadron Seven, the rescue flight of June 19, 1968, will always be acclaimed as one of the most daring feats of flying to come out of the Vietnam Conflict.

LT Lassen became the first naval aviator and fifth Navy man to be awarded the Medal of Honor for bravery in Vietnam.

He received the Congressional Medal of Honor:

For conspicuous gallantry and intrepidity at the risk of his life above and beyond the call of duty on 19 June 1968 as pilot and aircraft commander of a search and rescue helicopter, attached to Helicopter Support Squadron Seven, Detachment One Hundred Four, embarked in USS Preble (DLG 15), during operations against enemy forces in North Vietnam. Launched shortly after midnight to attempt the rescue of two downed aviators, Lieutenant (then

Lieutenant, Junior Grade) Lassen skillfully piloted his aircraft over unknown and hostile terrain to a steep, tree-covered hill on which the survivors had been located. Although enemy fire was being directed at the helicopter, he initially landed in a clear area near the base of the hill, but, due to the dense under-growth, the survivors could not reach the helicopter. With the aid of flare illu-mination, Lieutenant Lassen successfully accomplished a hover between two trees at the survivor's position. Illumination was abruptly lost as the last of the flares were expended, and the helicopter collided with a tree, commencing a sharp descent. Expertly righting his aircraft and maneuvering clear, Lieutenant Lassen remained in the area, determined to make another rescue attempt, and encouraged the downed aviators while awaiting resumption of flare illumina-tion. After another unsuccessful, illuminated, rescue attempt, and with his fuel dangerously low and his aircraft significantly damaged, he launched again and commenced another approach in the face of the continuing enemy opposition. When flare illumination was again lost, Lieutenant Lassen, fully aware of the dangers in clearly revealing his position to the enemy, turned on his landing lights and completed the landing. On this attempt, the survivors were able to make their way to the helicopter. Enroute to the coast, Lieutenant Lassen encountered and successfully evaded additional hostile antiaircraft fire and, with fuel for only five minutes of flight remaining, landed safely aboard USS Jouett (DLG 29). His courageous and daring actions, determination, and extraordinary airmanship in the face of great risk sustain and enhance the finest traditions of the United States Naval Service.

USS Clyde Everett Lassen (DDG-82), an Arleigh Burke class guided missile destroyer was named in honor of LT Lassen. It was commissioned on April 21, 2001.

William L. McGonagle, CAPT

Captain William L. McGonagle, U.S. Navy, was the Commanding Officer of the USS Liberty (AGTR-5) in International waters in the Eastern Mediterranean on 8-9 June 1967.

Captain McGonagle is one of my favorite MOH heroes. He did what he could do to save his unarmed ship from the strafing and bombing from the knowing all Israeli Defense Forces. I have my own personal and professional opinion on this episode. I was a telecommunications specialist in the Navy and had a chance to work with Navy spooks over the years. The Israeli Defense Forces knew that the USS Liberty was off the Sinai Peninsula and they knew it was a spook ship. They did not want the U.S. to monitor their communications during the conflict. So how do you make that happen? You take the USS Liberty out so they could no longer monitor their communications. It was a deliberate attack. I would like to see the Israelis come clean on this incident and tell the truth. I support the Israelis in trying to survive in a volatile area, but I feel they need to be truthful about the USS Liberty.

(The information below in quotations and italics was obtained from the USS Liberty website and all information is of public domain and can be obtained through the Freedom of Information Act.)

"Captain McGonagle received the Congressional Medal of Honor for his heroic actions while on routine patrol off the Sinai Peninsula in 1967 during the Israeli/Arab Six Day War when it was attacked by the armed forces of Israel. Thirty-four young American men gave their lives defending the USS Liberty against a sustained Israeli air and sea attack. The American intelligence ship USS Liberty was attacked for 75 minutes in international waters by Israeli aircraft and motor torpedo boats. Besides the 34 men who gave their lives, 171 others were wounded. Surprisingly, there has never been a complete and comprehensive public Congressional investigation though it is considered the only naval incident of its kind in American history.

"What we are seeking is to have that recognition removed from us and to have us treated exactly the same as every other US military unit which has been similarly attacked," Joe Meadors said, one of two signalmen aboard the Liberty. "I do have hope that we will get our chance to testify before Congress," John Hrankowski, a fireman for the carrier, concurred. "There are too many people coming out from that era and now telling what really happened that June 8th day." Israel still insists

that they mistook the Liberty for the out-of-service Egyptian supply vessel El Quseir. After all, the Liberty and El Quseir both had a single smokestack in midship. But that's where the similarity ends. The Liberty was not only significantly larger than El Quseir, but Jim Ennes, who was Officer-of-the-Deck at the time, said both the deckhouse arrangement and profile were different. The Court of Inquiry even noted that "if Liberty could be mistaken for El Quseir, then any coastal freighter in the world was in danger," Ennes said.

The Liberty also displayed a bright, clean American flag. That flag is on display at the National Crypto-logic Museum in Fort Meade, Maryland. The argument of "friendly fire" has been given. But survivors say this reasoning doesn't wash as the attack occurred on a clear afternoon, after 13 reconnaissance over-flights were made. Israeli intelligence even admitted, prior to the outbreak, of knowing "the exact location of all opposition forces and equipment—military and civilian.

"One should also consider Israeli air force intelligence General Yeshuah Bareket's comments during a Thames Television documentary concerning the Liberty attack: "The ship is an obstacle or is disturbing our operations in the area." In addition to the subsequent attack by planes, torpedo boats and helicopters, the Israelis also bombed the Liberty with napalm and shells. A total of 821 rocket and machine-gun holes were later reportedly counted in the Liberty's hull.

Could it still have been a "tragic case of misidentification" as Israel insists? Or was the attack launched to prevent the US from finding out about the killing of Egyptian POWs nearby? A congressional investigation might finally shed light on this.

Ennes, also author of the 1980 best-selling "Assault on the Liberty" clearly hopes for a congressional inquiry though he is disappointed with Congress. Israel persuaded "the US Congress to accept their version of the attack without even considering the eyewitness accounts of survivors," Ennes said. "That is a first in US history." The other first came when USS Liberty Captain William McGonagle became the only living recipient to have received his Congressional Medal of Honor for valor by an official other than our president.

So why hasn't there been an honest and open congressional investigation? Well, some Israelis insist that there have been five such investigations. Indeed, Senators John McCain, Ted Kennedy, Tim Wirth, and Congressmen Hank Brown and Larry Hopkins all assigned a staff person to inquire into the circumstances. But a legislator assigning a staff person to look into the details is not the same as the US Congress conducting a full-fledged investigation.

Captain McGonagle received the Congressional Medal of Honor:

For conspicuous gallantry and intrepidity at the risk of his life above and beyond the call of duty. Sailing in international waters, the Liberty was attacked without warning by jet fighter aircraft and motor torpedo boats which inflicted many casualties among the crew and caused extreme damage to the ship. Although severely wounded during the first air attack, Capt. McGonagle remained at his battle station on the badly damaged bridge and, with full knowledge of the seriousness of his wounds, subordinated his own welfare to the safety and survival of his command. Steadfastly refusing any treatment which would take him away from his post, he calmly continued to exercise firm command of his ship. Despite continuous exposure to fire, he maneuvered his ship, directed its defense, supervised the control of flooding and fire, and saw to the care of the casualties. Capt. McGonagle's extraordinary valor under these conditions inspired the surviving members of the Liberty's crew, many of them seriously wounded, to heroic efforts to overcome the battle damage and keep the ship afloat. Subsequent to the attack, although in great pain and weak from the loss of blood, Captain McGonagle remained at his battle station and continued to command his ship for more than 17 hours. It was only after rendezvous with a U.S. destroyer that he relinquished personal control of the Liberty and permitted himself to be removed from the bridge. Even then, he refused much needed medical attention until convinced that the seriously wounded among his crew had been treated. Capt. McGonagle's superb professionalism, courageous fighting spirit, and valiant leadership saved his ship and many lives. His actions sustain and enhance the finest traditions of the U.S. Naval Service.

Note: Captain McGonagle earned the Medal of Honor for actions that took place in international waters in the Eastern Mediterranean rather than in Vietnam.

Thomas R. Norris, LT and Michael E. Thornton, LT

Thomas R. Norris, Lieutenant (then LTJG), U.S. Navy, SEAL Advisor was assigned to Strategic Technical Directorate Assistance Team, Headquarters, U.S. Military Assistance Command., Quang Tri Province, Republic of Vietnam on 10 to 13 April 1972.

Michael Edwin Thornton, Lieutenant (then Engineman Second Class Petty Officer), U.S. Navy was assigned to the Navy Advisory Group., Republic of Vietnam, 31 October 1972.

These two men served together on a SEAL team in Vietnam. LT Norris received his Medal of Honor for an action six months prior to the action that got LT Thornton his MOH.

LTJG Norris was involved in the rescue of American pilots behind enemy lines while assigned as a SEAL Team Advisor in Quang Tri Province. The movie "BAT-21" starring Danny Glover and Gene Hackman was based on one of his rescues. After researching this incident and then going back and watching the movie, I can tell that the movie was vaguely based on the true actions of LTJG Norris who did receive his MOH for the rescue of the pilot of BAT-21.

Later in the year, Engineman Second Class Petty Officer Thornton was assigned to a pilot rescue operation with LTJG Norris along with an inexperienced South Vietnamese Navy officer and two veteran South Vietnamese Navy enlisted frogmen.

Thornton was privy to LTJG Norris' actions six months before. The team was inserted north of where they were supposed to be inserted for the rescue mission. When the found they were too far north, they began to back track to the beach to get their raft. Before they made it to the last sand dune, the North Vietnamese spotted them and opened fire. One South Vietnamese enlisted frogman was wounded in the leg. A shrapnel from a grenade opened wounds on Thornton's legs and his back. LTJG Norris was seriously injured. The South Vietnamese Navy officer thought he was dead and told Thornton that.

Thornton was not leaving without his lieutenant. No SEAL would ever be left behind by a brother. Thornton recovered his lieutenant who had a serious head wound, the skin laid back to reveal the white of his broken skull. His lieutenant was not moving. He was unconscious, but still alive.

Thornton made for the beach with the lieutenant's limp body draped over his shoulder with the enemy firing at them. Luckily neither was hit. When they reached the water at the beach, he continued on and dragged the lieutenant with him trying to keep his head above water. They were rescued two hours later by the same junk that had inserted them into the wrong place.

For his refusal to leave the wounded lieutenant behind and his courage in returning under fire to recover the fellow SEAL, Mike Thornton was recommended for the Medal of Honor. His action was the LAST Medal of Honor action of the Vietnam War, and the last by any living American until Operation Desert Shield.

Both LT Norris and LT Thornton received a Medal of Honor. There citations are as follows:

Lieutenant Thomas R. Norris received the Congressional Medal of Honor:

For conspicuous gallantry and intrepidity in action at the risk of his life above and beyond the call of duty while serving as a SEAL Advisor with the Strategic Technical Directorate Assistance Team, Headquarters, U.S. Military Assistance Command, Vietnam. During the period 10 to 13 April 1972, Lieutenant Norris completed an unprecedented ground rescue of two downed pilots deep within heavily controlled enemy territory in Quang Tri Province. Lieutenant Norris, on the night of 10 April, led a five-man patrol through 2,000 meters of heavily controlled enemy territory, located one of the downed pilots at daybreak, and returned to the Forward Operating Base (FOB). On 11 April, after a devastating mortar and rocket attack on the small FOB, Lieutenant Norris led a three man team on two unsuccessful rescue attempts for the second pilot. On the afternoon of the 12th, a Forward Air Controller located the pilot and notified Lieutenant Norris. Dressed in fishermen disguises and using a sampan, Lieutenant Norris and one Vietnamese traveled throughout that night and found the injured pilot at dawn. Covering the pilot with bamboo and vegetation, they began the return journey, successfully evading a North Vietnamese patrol. Approaching the FOB, they came under heavy machine gun fire. Lieutenant Norris called in an air strike which provided suppression fire and a smoke screen, allowing the rescue party to reach the FOB. By his outstanding display of decisive leadership, undaunted courage, and selfless dedication in the face of extreme danger, Lieutenant Norris enhanced the finest traditions of the United States Naval Service.

Engineman Second Class Michael E. Thornton received the Congressional Medal of Honor:

For conspicuous gallantry and intrepidity at the risk of his life above and beyond the call of duty while participating in a daring operation against enemy forces in the Republic of Vietnam on October 31, 1972. Petty Officer Thornton, an assistant U.S. Navy advisor, along with a U.S. Navy lieutenant serving as senior advisor, accompanied a three-man Vietnamese Navy SEAL patrol on an intelligence gathering and prisoner capture operation against an enemy-occupied naval river base. Launched from a Vietnamese Navy junk in a rubber boat, the patrol reached land and was continuing on foot toward its objective when it suddenly came under heavy fire from a numerically superior force. The patrol called in naval gunfire support and then engaged the enemy in a fierce firefight, accounting for many enemy casualties before moving back to the waterline to prevent encirclement. Upon learning that the senior advisor had been hit by enemy fire and was believed to be dead, Petty Officer Thornton returned through a hail of fire to the lieutenant's last position, quickly disposed of two enemy soldiers about to overrun the position, and succeeded in removing the seriously wounded and unconscious senior naval advisor to the water's edge. He then inflated the lieutenant's life jacket and towed him seaward for approximately two hours until picked up by support craft. By his extraordinary courage and perseverance, Petty Officer Thornton was directly responsible for saving the life of his superior officer and enabling the safe extraction of all patrol members, thereby upholding the highest traditions of the United States Naval Service.

David G. Ouellet, SN

David G. Ouellet was a U.S. Navy Seaman assigned to River Squadron 5, My Tho Detachment 532, Mekong River, Republic of Vietnam on 6 March 1967.David George Ouellet was born in Newton, Massachusetts, on June 13, 1944, son of Chester J. and Elizabeth E. Ouellet. He graduated from Hardy School, Wellesley, Massachusetts, in 1958; attended Wellesley Junior High School; and subsequently was employed by the Alfred Fisher Trucking Company in Wellesley. On July 28, 1964, he enlisted in the U.S. Navy at Boston, Massachusetts, and had recruit training at the Naval Training Center, Great Lakes, Illinois. Completing his training in October 1964, he joined Assault Craft Division TWELVE, and while attached to that division served for five months in 1965 in the Vietnam era.

Between June and August 1966 he had river patrol boat training at the Naval Schools Command, Vallejo, California, after which he had training at the Naval Amphibious Base, Coronado, California. On September 21, 1966 he reported for duty with River Squadron FIVE and was attached to My Tho Detachment 532 of that squadron and at the time of his death on March 6, 1967.

He received the Congressional Medal of Honor posthumously:

For conspicuous gallantry and intrepidity at the risk of his life above and beyond the call of duty while serving with River Section 532, in combat against the enemy in the Republic of Vietnam. As the forward machine gunner on River Patrol Boat (PBR) 124, which was on patrol on the Mekong River during the early evening hours of 6 March 1967, Seaman Ouellet observed suspicious activity near the river bank, alerted his Boat Captain, and recommended movement of the boat to the area to investigate. While the PBR was making a high-speed run along the river bank, Seaman Ouellet spotted an incoming enemy grenade falling toward the boat. He immediately left the protected position of his gun mount and ran aft for the full length of the speeding boat, shouting to his fellow crew members to take cover. Observing the Boat Captain standing unprotected on the boat, Seaman Ouellet bounded onto the engine compartment cover, and pushed the Boat Captain down to safety. In the split second that followed the grenade's landing, and in the face of certain death, Seaman Ouellet fearlessly placed himself between the deadly missile and his shipmates, courageously absorbing most of the blast fragments with his own body in order to protect his shipmates from injury and death. His extraordinary heroism and his selfless and courageous actions on behalf of his comrades at the expense of his own life were in the finest tradition of the United States Naval Service.

USS OUELLET (FF-1077) was the first ship of the United States Navy to bear the name of Seaman David George Ouellet. It was one of a class of frigates specifically designated to locate and destroy enemy submarines.

OUELLET's keel was laid at Avondale Shipyard Incorporated in Westwego, Louisiana on January 15, 1969. She was christened at Charleston Naval Shipyard, South Carolina on December 12, 1970. OUELLET arrived at her homeport in Pearl Harbor, Hawaii on April 15, 1971, with her first deployment to the Western Pacific commencing on January 27, 1972. OUELLET twice came under hostile fire during this deployment, however no causalities were sustained.

During ceremonies re-establishing the U.S. Third Fleet on February 1, 1973, USS OUELLET became the first Third Fleet flagship since World War II.

David R. Ray, HM2

David R. Ray was a U.S. Navy Hospital Corpsman Second Class assigned to 2nd Battalion, 11th Marines, 1st Marine Division (Rein), FMF, Quang Nam Province, Republic of Vietnam on 19 March 1969.The son of Mr. and Mrs. David F. Ray, he was born on 14 February 1945 in McMinnville Tennessee. He graduated from City High School in McMinnville in 1963. David R. Ray was a 1963 University of Tennessee alumni scholarship winner and attended university's Knoxville campus from 1963 to 1966. He enlisted in the U.S. Navy at Nashville, Tennessee on 28 March 1966 and subsequently reported to Recruit Training Command Naval Training San Diego, after which he was assigned to the Naval Hospital in the USS HAVINN (AH 12). Following his tour in the hospital ship, David next served at Naval Hospital Long Beach, California.

In Mays 1968 he requested a tour of duty with the Marines. He reported for instruction at Field Medical Service School, Marine Corps Base, Camp Pendleton, California in July he joined Second Battalion, Eleventh Marines, First Marine Division (Reinforced), Fleet Marine Force.

David R. Ray was serving as a corpsman with the battalion when he was mortally wounded on 19 March 1969, while treating wounded Marines "For conspicuous gallantry at the risk of his life above and beyond the call of duty…near An Hoa, Quang Nam Province, in the Republic of Vietnam…" David Robert Ray was posthumously awarded the Medal of Honor. In addition to the Purple Heart Medal which was awarded for wounds received in action, he also had the Combat Action Ribbon, National Defense Medal, Vietnam Service Medal with star, and the Republic of Vietnam Campaign Medal.

He received the Congressional Medal of Honor posthumously:

For conspicuous gallantry and intrepidity at the risk of his life above and beyond the call of duty while serving as a corpsman with Battery D, 2d Battalion, 11th Marines, 1st Marine Division, at Phu Loc 6, near An Hoa, Quang Nam Province, in the Republic of Vietnam, on 19 March 1969. During the early morning hours, an estimated battalion-sized enemy force launched a determined assault against the Battery's position, and succeeded in effecting a penetration of the barbed-wire perimeter. The initial burst of enemy fire caused numerous casualties among the Marines who had immediately manned their howitzers during the rocket and mortar attack. Undaunted by the intense hostile fire, Petty Officer Ray moved from parapet to parapet, rendering emergency medical treatment to the wounded. Although seriously wounded himself while administering first aid to a Marine casualty, he refused medical aid and continued his life saving efforts. While he was bandaging and attempting to comfort another wounded Marine, Petty Officer Ray was forced to battle two enemy soldiers who attacked his position, personally killing one and wounding the other. Rapidly losing his strength as a result of his own severe wounds, he nonetheless managed to move through the hail of enemy fire to other casualties. Once again, he was faced with the intense fire of oncoming enemy troops and, despite the grave personal danger and insurmountable odds, succeeded in treating the wounded and holding off the enemy until he ran out of ammunition, at which time he sustained fatal wounds. Petty Officer Ray's final act of heroism was to protect the patient he was treating. He threw himself upon the wounded Marine, thus saving the man's life when an enemy grenade exploded nearby. By his determined and persevering actions, courageous spirit, and selfless devotion to the welfare of his Marine comrades, Petty Officer Ray served to inspire the men of Battery D to heroic efforts in defeating the enemy. His conduct throughout was in keeping with the finest traditions of the United States Naval Service.

USS DAVID R. RAY (DD-972) was the ninth SPRUANCE-class destroyer and was named in memory of HM3 Ray. USS DAVID R. RAY was commissioned on November 19, 1977 and decommissioned February 28, 2002.

Marvin G. Shields, CM3

Marvin G. Shields was a U.S. Navy Seabee Construction Mechanic Third Class assigned to Seabee Team 1104, Dong Xoai, Republic of Vietnam on 10 June 1965.Marvin G. Shields, born 30 December 1939 in Port Townsend, Wash., enlisted in the Navy 8 January 1962. After construction training, he served with Mobile Construction Battalion 11, and was with Seabee Team 1104 at Dong Xoai, South Vietnam, 10 June 1965 when a Vietcong regiment attacked. After being wounded, Shields continued to carry up ammunition to the firing line, and after receiving a second wound, insisted on helping a more severely wounded soldier to safety. Refusing to consider himself and now greatly weakened, he again exposed himself to enemy fire, volunteering to help knock out a machine-gun which had the entire camp pinned down. Shields died from wounds he received after he and others "succeeded in destroying the enemy machine gun emplacement, thus undoubtedly saving the lives of many of their fellow servicemen in the compound."

He received the Congressional Medal of Honor posthumously:

For conspicuous gallantry and intrepidity at the risk of his life above and beyond the call of duty while serving with United States Navy Seabee Team 1104 at Dong Xoai, Republic of Vietnam, on 10 June 1965. Although wounded when the compound of Detachment A-342, 5th Special Forces Group (Airborne), 1st Special Forces, came under intense fire from an estimated reinforced Viet Cong regiment employing machine gun, heavy weapons and small arms, Shields continued to resupply his fellow Americans with needed ammunition and to return the enemy fire for a period of approximately three hours, at which time the Viet Cong launched a massive attack at close range with flame throwers, hand grenades and small-arms fire. Wounded a second time during this attack, Shields nevertheless assisted in carrying a more critically wounded man to safety, and then resumed firing at the enemy for four more hours. When the Commander asked for a volunteer to accompany him in an attempt to knock out an enemy machine gun emplacement which was endangering the lives of all personnel in the compound because of the accuracy of its fire, Shields unhesitatingly volunteered for this extremely hazardous mission. Proceeding toward their objective with a 3.5-inch rocket launcher, they succeeded in destroying the enemy machine gun emplacement, thus undoubtedly saving the lives of many of their fellow servicemen in the compound. Shields was mortally wounded by hostile fire while returning to his defensive position.

His heroic initiative and great personal valor in the face of intense enemy fire sustain and enhance the finest tradition of the United States Naval Service.

USS Marvin Shields (FF-1066) was named in memory of CM3 Shields and was commissioned on April 10, 1971 and decommissioned on July 2, 1992.

James B. Stockdale, Vice Admiral

James B. Stockdale, Vice Admiral (then Captain), a U.S. Navy pilot, while serving as senior POW in Hoa Lo prison, Hanoi, North Vietnam on 4 September 1969. Vice Admiral Stockdale is my all time favorite hero in the Navy. He served on active duty in the regular Navy for 37 years, most of those years as a fighter pilot aboard aircraft carriers. Shot down on his third combat tour over North Vietnam, he was the senior naval prisoner of war in Hanoi for seven and one-half years, tortured 15 times, in solitary confinement for over four years, in leg irons for two. When physical disability from combat wounds brought about Stockdale's military retirement, he had the distinction of being the only three-star officer in the history of the U.S. Navy to wear both aviator wings and the Medal of Honor. Admiral Stockdale was one of the most decorated Naval officers in the history of the U.S. Navy. Included in his 26 other combat decorations are two Distinguished Flying Crosses, three Distinguished Service Medals, four Silver Star medals, and two Purple Hearts. Vice Admiral Stockdale became a vice presidential candidate as Ross Perot's running mate in 1996. He passed away from complications of Alzheimer's disease in 2005.

He received the Congressional Medal of Honor: For conspicuous gallantry and intrepidity at the risk of his life above and beyond the call of duty on 4 September 1969 while senior naval officer in the Prisoner of War camps of North Vietnam. Recognized by his captors as the leader in the Prisoners, of War resistance to interrogation and in their refusal to participate in propaganda exploitation, Rear Admiral (then Captain) Stockdale was singled out for interrogation and attendant torture after he was detected in a covert communications attempt. Sensing the start of another purge, and aware that his earlier efforts at self-disfiguration to dissuade his captors from exploiting him for propaganda purposes had resulted in cruel and agonizing punishment, Rear Admiral Stockdale resolved to make himself a symbol of resistance regardless of personal sacrifice. He deliberately inflicted a near-mortal wound to his person in order to convince his captors of his willingness to give up his life rather than capitulate. He was subsequently discovered and revived by the North Vietnamese who, convinced of his indomitable spirit, abated in their employment of excessive harassment and torture toward all of the Prisoners of War. By his heroic action, at great peril to himself, he earned the everlasting gratitude of his fellow prisoners and of his country. Rear Admiral Stockdale's valiant leadership and extraordinary courage in a hostile environment sustained enhance the finest traditions of the United States Naval Service.

On January 12, 2006, the Department of Defense announced that DDG hull number 106 would be named in honor of Vice Adm. James Bond Stockdale (1923-2005), the legendary leader of American prisoners of war (POWs) during the Vietnam War.

The USS Stockdale (DDG-106) will be a Flight IIA variant of the Arleigh Burke-class guided-missile destroyer and will incorporate a helicopter hanger facility into the original design. The ship can carry two SH-60B/R Light Airborne Multipurpose System MK III helicopters.

Guided-missile destroyers operate independently and in conjunction with carrier battle groups, surface action groups, amphibious groups and replenishment groups.

James E. Williams, BM1

James E. Williams, Boatswain's Mate First Class Petty Officer, was assigned to River Section 531, My Tho, RVN, Mekong River, Republic of Vietnam, 31 October 1966.Skillful battle direction is one of the most important require-ments for a leader in the U.S. Navy. Boatswain's Mate 1st Class James E. Williams, who received the Medal of Honor for his achievements, demon-strated extraordinary bravery and leadership during the Vietnam War. The petty officer was assigned to the River Patrol Force whose mission was to inter-cept Viet Cong arms shipments on the waterways of South Vietnam's Mekong Delta.

He was the most highly decorated enlisted man in the history of the U.S. Navy. On May 14, 1968 the President of the United States, in the name of Congress, presented him the Medal of Honor. His other awards include the Navy Cross, Silver Star (2 awards), Legion of Merit (with Combat V), Navy and Marine Corp Medal (2 awards), Bronze Star (3 Awards), Vietnam Cross of Gallantry with Gold Star and Palm, Navy Commendation Medal, Presidential Unit Citation (2 awards), Purple Heart (3 awards), Vietnam Service Medal (1 star), Republic of Vietnam Campaign Medal, National Defense Service Medal (1 star), United Nations Service Medal, Korean Service Medal (2 stars), Korean Presidential Unit Citation and Good Conduct Medal (5 awards).

On 31 October 1966, Williams, patrol commander for his boat, River Patrol Boat 105, and another PBR was searching for Viet Cong guerrillas operating in an isolated area of the Delta. Suddenly, Communist guerrillas manning two sampans opened fire on the Americans. When Williams and his men neutral-ized one boat crew, the other one escaped into a nearby canal. The PBR sailors gave chase and soon found themselves in a beehive of enemy activity as Viet Cong guerrillas opened up with rocket propelled grenades and small arms against the Americans from fortified river bank positions. Against overwhelm-ing odds, several times Williams led his PBRs against concentrations of enemy junks and sampans. He also called for support from the heavily armed UH-1B Huey helicopters of Navy Helicopter Attack (Light) Squadron 3, the "Seawolves." When that help arrived, he kicked off another attack in the failing light, cleverly turning on his boats' searchlights to illuminate enemy forces and positions. As a result of the three-hour battle, the American naval force killed numerous Viet Cong guerrillas, destroyed over fifty vessels, and disrupted a major enemy logistic operation. BM1 Williams not only displayed great courage under fire, but a keen understanding of how his Sailors, weapons, and equipment could be used to achieve victory.

He retired from active service in 1967.

He received the Congressional Medal of Honor:

For conspicuous gallantry and intrepidity at the risk of his life above and beyond the call of duty as a member of River Section 531 during combat operations on the Mekong River in the Republic of Vietnam. On 31 October 1966, Petty Officer Williams was serving as Boat Captain and Patrol Officer aboard River Patrol Boat (PBR) 105 accompanied by another patrol boat when the patrol was suddenly taken under fire by two enemy sampans. Petty Officer Williams immediately ordered the fire returned, killing the crew of one enemy boat and causing the other sampan to take refuge in a nearby river inlet. Pursuing the fleeing sampan, the U.S. patrol encountered a heavy volume of small arms fire from enemy forces, at close range, occupying well-concealed positions along the river bank. Maneuvering through this fire, the patrol confronted a numerically superior enemy force aboard two enemy junks and eight sampans augmented by heavy automatic weapons fire from ashore. In the savage battle that ensued, Petty Officer Williams, with utter disregard for his own safety, exposed himself to the withering hail of enemy fire to direct counter fire and inspire the actions of his patrol. Recognizing the overwhelming strength of the enemy force, Petty Officer Williams deployed his patrol to await the arrival of armed helicopters. In the course of this movement he discovered an even larger concentration of enemy boats. Not waiting for the arrival of the armed helicopters, he displayed great initiative and boldly led the patrol through the intense enemy fire and damaged or destroyed fifty enemy sampans and seven junks. This phase of the action completed, and with the arrival of the armed helicopters, Petty Officer Williams directed the attack on the remaining enemy force. Now virtually dark, and although Petty Officer Williams was aware that his boats would become even better targets, he ordered the patrol boats' search lights turned on to better illuminate the area and moved the patrol perilously close to shore to press the attack. Despite a waning supply of ammunition the patrol successfully engaged the enemy ashore and completed the rout of the enemy force. Under the leadership of Petty Officer Williams, who demonstrated unusual professional skill and indomitable courage throughout the three hour battle, the patrol accounted for the destruction or loss of sixty-five enemy boats and inflicted numerous casualties on the enemy personnel. His extraordinary heroism and exemplary fighting spirit in the face of grave risks inspired the efforts of his men to defeat a larger enemy force, and are in keeping with the finest traditions of the United States Naval Service.

USS James E. Williams (DDG-95) was named in memory of BM1 James E. Williams and is an Arleigh Burke class guided-missile destroyer. The Williams was christened on June 28, 2003 at Northrop Grumman Ship Systems in Pascagoula, Miss. Acting Secretary of the Navy Hansford T. Johnson, deliver the ceremony's principal address. Mrs. Elaine W. Williams, widow of the ship's namesake, served as ship's sponsor. James E. Williams was commissioned on Dec. 11, 2004, at Naval Weapons Station's Wharf Alpha. U.S. Senator Lindsey Graham delivered the ceremony's principal address. Elaine Weaver Williams, widow of the ship's namesake, served as ship's sponsor.

Chapter 7

Middle East Experiences

I was the assistant communications officer on the USS Independence (CV-62) during Operation Desert Shield. It was an experience that I am glad that I had. Included in this chapter are a couple of stories, one by a Chief Petty Officer, who became ill after his stint of duty there and my own personal story of flying around that region during the first part of Desert Shield.

"War should be the politics of last resort. And when we go to war, we should have a purpose that our people understand and support."
—Colin Powell, U.S. Secretary of State

Operation Desert Shield/Desert Storm Casualties—148 KIA, 145 non-combat related deaths, 467 wounded

War on Terror Casualties:

Operation Enduring Freedom (Afghanistan)—124 KIA (including 4 CIA officers), 363 wounded (as of book publishing date)

Operation Iraqi Freedom (Iraq)—1752 KIA, 257 non-combat related deaths, 7,592 wounded (as of book publishing date)

Tracings in the Sand
By Mark Bell

I served in Operation Desert Shield/Desert Storm as a Navy Intelligence Specialist from December 1990-December 1991. I was assigned to USS LaSalle AGF-3, forward deployed with a Cryptologic Direct Support Element (CDSE) on the USS Tripoli (Onboard during Mine Strike), USS Missouri (Onboard during CSSC-3 Silkworm Missile Attack), and USS Wisconsin. I was on other ships but for less than a week so the above are the ones I remember the most. I was also onshore at the Kuwaiti Children's Hospital, and the Holiday Inn site and the "mile of death".

The smell of high explosives in the air was mixed with that of paint, thinner, and sea water. It was pitch black and I was sure I was dead. As I lay on the deck trying to regain my sense of reality and life I slowly started to feel the pain in my right side and shoulder. I found my flashlight on my belt and turned it on. There was smoke and dust in the air. I was alone in an isolated passageway just above the compartment where an Iraqi sea mine had just put a 20 X 30 foot hole in our ship, the USS Tripoli.

There was no time for pain, thoughts of dying, or panic. I picked myself up off the floor and found my way to the Intelligence Space where I was assigned. Upon entering I realized my shipmate was not there (as he should have been since GQ had sounded). I told my LT I was going to check his rack. I found him in his rack in shock. He could not talk and clutched his pillow to his chest crying. I told him all would be O.K. because we had the training to overcome this. He was unable to leave his rack and I went back to the Intel center. I began to destroy our classified materials and keying materials. All the systems on the ship were out, the emergency generator was hit in the explosion and it was not functional. One of the CTMs and I were able to get the Long Range SPRAC (radio) working with a 12 volt battery and the Captain made his call to the Admiral in Bahrain. For the next four days no one was spared, we all worked 24/7 to keep the ship afloat and show the world you can not defeat the spirit of Liberty and Peace. On day four I flew off the ship to the USS Missouri to continue our much needed mission.

Upon arrival we supplemented the RPV targeting team. We would send the RPVs out to coordinates where intelligence indicated targets existed worthy of

16 inch gunfire interdiction. As the RPVs flew over a target we would make a call on the worthiness of the target. We then targeted the guns and destroyed the target. We watched the shells hit target after target where hundreds upon hundreds of Iraqi soldiers were. We realized the death and destruction was necessary to prepare the way for our troops to move up and retake Kuwait. I felt a sense of sorrow for the brave Iraqi soldiers who died because of our shells. I felt it could have easily have been me. Then the 1MC (ships intercom) sounded the alarm…"Brace for shock, missile inbound"…no one had to tell those of us in the RPV/intelligence space what was coming, we knew all to well the CSSC-3 Silkworm missile site we were looking for found us first. Silkworm missiles can penetrate 40 inches of steel plate armor. The USS Missouri had 18" at its thickest spot. We were located on the Bridge Wing just below the helm: we also knew the profile of a silkworm and we were the "target within the target" Then on the radio monitoring system the HMS Gloucester said, Sea Dart away (anti-missile missile) then just as quickly, "Sea Dart missed, second Sea Dart away". I looked at the ISCS beside me, he was crying. I felt for sure I was living my last few seconds of my life, I tried to imagine what the explosion would be like…would it be like the explosion on the USS Tripoli was a few days before? Would I be incinerated or torn apart by flying metal fragments of the ship. How fragile I felt at that moment. I thought of my wife and children, I said a quick prayer for them and was ready to die. Then the radio reported, "Missile intercepted second missile inbound, brace for shock". Then a few moments later the all clear was sounded. During this time other things were happening as well. We heard projectiles hitting the skin of the ship just outside the compartment. it turned out that we took friendly fire the same time as the missile attack. Our self defenses were all shut down except for the "Chaff Launchers". The self-defense systems can not stand the shock of the 16" gun fire. When the missile was headed for the Missouri our Chaff launchers were set off to distract the missile if it was doing terminal targeting; however, it attracted the "Sea Wiz" close in weapons system of a nearby friendly ship and we were hit by its fire of depleted uranium.

I still can't talk about what I experienced ashore in Kuwait City but will say anyone there knows how we found many of the Kuwaiti resistance and how we found the children in the Kuwaiti Children's Hospital. The death and bodies still haunt me at nights. The smell of death will never leave me. God bless the Sri Lankan nurses we helped or did they help us deal with the children's deaths?

The mile of death has been covered by others…there is nothing I can add.
My R&R finally came and I was put on the USS LaSalle when she left the Kuwait City port. We were to sail to Oman, Mina Quaboos and have some time

off. The trip down there was uneventful. We had a great time in Oman. Then we started back through the Strait of Hormuz. The Iraqi Republican Guard Corps (IRGC) were waiting and ambushed us with several Boghammer (small) boats. The AK-47 fire was heavy and when the Captain called down to the Intel center to ask who it was, the IRGC was the answer I gave him who were the only known hostiles in the area. We returned fire and killed several of the IRGC and damaged many of their boats, they fled into the night. It was tense for several hours. The "sound of freedom" jets from the USS Kennedy were overhead shortly after the attack (15-20 min); it seemed an eternity. The next few hours saw the entire Iraqi fleet get underway and head for our location. We offered assistance when they arrived but they refused our assistance saying, "I think you have done enough". So much for Rest and Relaxation!

At the end of my tour I helped put together the Intel center at ASU in Manama, Bahrain. Then I was transferred to Italy to help in the Yugoslavian war.

After the war, while stationed in Italy, I started experiencing symptoms of PTSD. One symptom is "workaholism". I threw myself into my work on the Yugo problem. But when I stopped for just a few hours, I would "feel" the "black fog" surrounding me and making my life impossible to live. I was nominated as "Sailor of the Year" and won.

Then in 1995 I decided to leave the service with 14 years of active duty. Both Admirals I briefed daily tried to talk me out of it. The Command Master Chief tried but "something" would not let me go on. I got out and was hired as a Narcotics Investigator in Oak Ridge, Tennessee. Once again, I threw myself into my work. I did well and was a very successful Narcotics officer. However, I became increasingly angry and depressed. I drank and my family life became violent. I even threatened my wife at one point. I had changed...180 degrees out. On several occasions when with my wife and kids in the car I would feel so unsafe and angry I would stop and run into the woods to a "safe place". The PTSD was in total control of my spirit, life and world. I also was experiencing fatigue, joint pain, nightmares, chest pain, and suicidal feelings.

Then at the end of 1998 I was recalled to active duty for Operation Desert Fox. I lucked out and was assigned to CENTCOM in Tampa, FL. Then, almost immediately, I was recalled involuntarily to service in SFOR, Bosnia. I was assigned to a HUMINT unit and worked from Jan 1999 to Aug 1999 in that unit. You may recall we were involved in the mission in Serbia/Kosovo. So was

I. All the mass graves, death, bombed out buildings, death threats, near capture on the Montenegro border, and other close calls finally pushed me over the edge. I had not slept in many months. After the last bomb fell in Serbia I waited four days and went to the combat stress control unit at Eagle Base in Tuzla; I was diagnosed for the first time in my life with PTSD. I was medically evacuated to Germany then the States.

There I was treated and discharged by medical board in April of 2001. I am rated by the VA at 80%. It has been a fight the whole way. I still suffer. I lost my family, (they will not let me live with them they are afraid of me) my job, my ability to support my family, and my health. That is my story.

Epilogue.—I wrote the "Tracings in the Sand" article in Sept of 2001. I felt then that people had this idea that during the first Gulf war we just walked in and asked for the keys to Kuwait and there was no fighting and there wasn't much of a war. For the proud Iraqis that died and for the men on the US led Collation we all know what happened there, and it wasn't as easy and bloodless as the press made it seem. Don't get me wrong. It needed to be done but as a professional military man I respected the fighting ability of the Iraqi considering the impossible odds they were up against.

We had a motto in one of my units, "Improvise, adapt and overcome!" The past several years have been the test of that motto. Many have said it and never had to use it; many can't say it but use it each day as they struggle to live a life with Post Traumatic Stress Disorder and the "leftovers of war".

Now for the rest of the story since Sept of 2001:

I had met a female Marine while at the Portsmouth Medical Center for treatment of my PTSD and awaiting discharge on medical grounds. One of the things PTSD does to a person is make them feel worthless and isolated from the rest of the world. I had few friends because of this. I had a vacuum that needed to be filled in my empty social life. So when Kathy (not her real name) came along and had experienced the same symptoms I had from PTSD, we became instant friends. (Her PTSD resulted from violence and an assault). It was an unhealthy relationship from the start because PTSD is hard enough to deal with when you don't have any problems but to put two people with PTSD together is explosive. It was, and to make a long story short, we both lived together for about eight months. The last two were Oct and Nov of 2001. In Nov of 2001, she committed suicide and I was at the bottom of life's barrel. Raw reality gripped me and I took a good hard look at myself. I was living in a $400.00 rented apartment in Upper State New York. My family didn't want anything to do with me. My "girlfriend" was now gone and I didn't know why I had been spared and had not died in Kuwait or on the ships during the attacks or in Kuwait City. I wished I had at that time. Then I picked up my Bible and found hope. I don't want to make this a "pitch" for Christianity, but without Christ I probably would have followed "Kathy" and committed suicide, also. Christ healed the wounds and gave me hope. That's all I will say right now about what Christ did for me because I know many have found what I just expressed to be true.

Knowing life had to go on and it was up to me to, improvise, adapt and overcome, I called my brother in Texas and made arrangements to move there so I would have the support of family nearby as I started my recovery and reintegration into society. My brother Jay and his wife Jan were great and being able to talk to them made life better and I felt less isolated. About December of 2001 when I was trying to evaluate my life I decided I needed a healthy relationship, someone that really loved me in spite of my problems (PTSD). I didn't know where to turn but one evening, on a lark, I signed up with an Internet dating service. I was very honest in my profile and thought only a deranged, self-abusive person would answer my ad! I did receive answers but turned them down because I didn't think they would be able to handle it. Then one girl wrote me and she was so honest and sweet…and wanted the same thing I wanted. Was this to good to be true? I had to see. So I made arrangements to visit her in Ontario, Canada where she lived. We had written for four months back and forth daily and I felt I knew her as well as one could know one without meeting. When we met it was "Love at first sight". We were married on 24 August 2002 in Greenville, SC and have never looked back! She has been my answer to prayer. Understanding, loving and now the mother of our son, Joshua, born Jan 25, 2004. What a difference she has made in my life. I still suffer from PTSD but having someone who has "made herself smart on PTSD", she helps me get through the tough spots in life. She helps me in so many ways like, helping me screen my e-mails and other things so I don't have to hit some triggers that would set my PTSD off. We now live in Sussex, New Brunswick and volunteer at the Circle Square Ranch, (a year-round Christian Camp). There she cooks in the kitchen and helps with the horse program, and I run the heavy equipment and do just about anything else that is needed. Recovery from the wars I was involved in is slow but at this point I can live a fairly normal life. I can't work a full time job and avoid news about the current wars. (I still wish I could be there helping out my fellow shipmates and soldiers). But I can live life with the help of God and my supportive wife and family!

Flying Around and Over The Persian Gulf
By Donald Johnson

USS Independence (CV-62) arrived on station in the Gulf of Oman on August 4, 1990 and launched a combat air patrol over northern Saudi Arabia as a deterrent to keep Saddam Hussein and his army from taking over the oil fields there. We were the tip of the spear and ready to go to war. We had a couple of pilots that pushed the envelope and were trying to draw the Iraqi pilots across the border so that they could practice their Top Gun training.

We had Commander, Carrier Group Three onboard commanded by Rear Admiral Jerry Unruh. I worked closely with his communicators in working out a telecommunications war time plan that would be the model for all aircraft carrier battle groups that would arrive in the Gulf.

The Indy was also the primary ship for all cryptographic equipment and key-ing material. We had an inventory of extra equipment and keying material that we could provide to other ships and ground units in the area. My CMS Custodian was a young ensign by the name of Dave Rausch. He was also a bridge watch stander. I was not. I had my fill of that while on the Belleau Wood.

We steamed in a square all day long launching aircraft for the combat air patrol. My radiomen were operating at top efficiency for the first time since I had come on board. I was feeling good about the department as a whole.

Within two weeks after arriving on station, we received a request from the British Army in Muscat, Oman for assistance to repair a couple of old trans-ceivers and antennas. An electronics technician Chief Warrant Officer, Patrick Maloney and I were probably the only two on board that knew anything about these transceivers. He and I both used to repair these things. We both arranged for a helo flight into Muscat so the Brits could pick us up and take us out to the communications facility. This would be the one and only trip to Muscat that I would get. The Brits met us at the airport and drove us out to their facility. It was great getting off the ship for a day. Patrick got a list of parts needed to repair the transceivers and antennas. We had lunch and a beer with the Brits. I shared my experience with British Grenadier soldiers in Hong Kong in 1976, a story I told in my last book. I told them that I knew why they needed our help in during war time. It took six of their best to take one American sailor out of action. They laughed at that. The Brits wore civilian clothes there so they did not stand out with their uniforms on. We had our uniforms on, so they tried their best to keep us low key. Warrant Maloney went back a few days later with one of his techs and one of my radiomen to do repairs.

Two people were required to pickup and deliver cryptographic equipment and keying material. Dave Rausch was not able to leave because of his bridge watch standing duties, so I ended up going with Senior Chief McNeese, my assistant CMS Custodian.

All cryptographic equipment and keying material was delivered from the states to a facility at the U.S. Naval Base in Bahrain. It was too far north in the Gulf to take a helo ride in. That was a COD (carrier onboard delivery) flight in a C-2 twin turboprop. The C-2 could carry cargo, passengers or a combination. I am not a great flying passenger. I am one of those who was very controlling and if I could not be in control of every situation in my life, I became a nervous wreck. Flying was one of those things that made me a nervous wreck.

The morning of the COD flight to Bahrain was here. We all embarked in the plane. We had to put on inflatable life vests and helmets. The passenger seats were all facing aft or pointed towards the rear of the plane. When the COD was ready for take off, it taxied over to the starboard side catapult. Once the catapult captain was ready, the COD braked and revved both engines all ahead full. Next thing I knew we were being catapulted forward. The force of the catapult forced me forward in the seat with the seat belt holding me and it felt like my eyeballs were popping out of my head. All of sudden I had a head rush. This was a first for me and the neatest thing I had done in many years. This was better than Space Mountain at Disneyland.

We arrived in Bahrain an hour and a half later. Senior Chief and I made our way over to the base CMS vault to find out what we had waiting for us. The COD was not leaving until the next day to go back to the ship, so we decided to leave the CMS material at the vault and went over to one of the base eateries to eat something different than shipboard food. We then checked in with base billeting to see if we could get a room for the night. They were booked so we had to go out in town. They recommended we stay at the International Regency.

We took a cab to the hotel, registered and got our rooms. I wanted to watch some TV. We had some American TV onboard ship with CNN which was our main news source with CBS, NBC and ABC being there as a back up. I wanted to read a Western newspaper. I got all of that at the hotel. Senior Chief and I planned to meet at the hotel bar at 1900 to have a couple of beers. What a surprise I got when I found out the beer was $7.00 US per pint. I drank $14.00 worth of beer and did not even get a buzz.

The hotel was full of what appeared to be military people in civilian clothes. Senior Chief and I brought one set of civilian clothes to put on just in case we had to go out into town. There were several Press Agents there. They had their badges on and were trying to get news by talking to the military people. I stayed clear of the Press.

The next morning we were up early, had breakfast in the hotel restaurant and headed back to the base. We retrieved our classified material and headed to the air field to catch the COD back to the Indy. The COD took off on schedule. Today would be another first for me. We had about 20 passengers and crew on this flight with a lot of cargo.

I was talking to Senior Chief trying to get to know the guy a little better. Then we started to descend so we could land on the Indy. We could not see anything and it is good that we couldn't. The C-2 was lined up and ready to land. I felt the plane hit the deck but then it accelerated and took off again. It flew out and came about again. It tried landing again and missed the last arresting cable for the second time. It once again accelerated and took off. The C-2 tried two more times with no success. On the fifth and final try the tailhook hooked onto the fourth arresting cable and we came to an abrupt stop. This was different than takeoff. The force of the stop pulled me into the back of the seat and my eyeballs felt as though they were trying to find the inside of my skull. One of the plane crew said that they were training a new pilot and this was his first landing. If he had missed on that landing we would have had to go back to Bahrain. The plane crew member said he was going to try not to fly with this guy again. I didn't want to either.

My next trip was a helo flight to the USNS Mercy, a hospital ship, sitting in the Persian Gulf. We had to deliver some keying material to them so they could communicate with the Navy battle groups and the battle field commanders if we went to war.

Once again, it was Senior Chief McNeese and myself delivering the material. We took off and landed on the flight deck of the Mercy about two hours later. The helo left us there and would be back to pick us up at 1400. We met up with the Chief Radioman and had him sign for the material. He then took us to lunch. Everyone ate in the same mess on board this ship. I had never seen so many pretty nurses and female doctors in one place. I got to talk to several of them when we sat down to eat. I had seen many of them when we landed sunbathing on the upper decks of the ship. I hadn't seen a good looking American girl in quite some time. I was enjoying what they call "eyeball liberty." The helo returned at about 1430 and returned us to the ship.

The final trip off the ship while in the Gulf was when the Indy actually went up into the Persian Gulf from the Gulf of Oman. This was going to be the first time in over 20 years that an aircraft carrier had gone into the Gulf. The Navy wanted to find out if an aircraft carrier could operate in the Gulf with its shallow and warm waters for an extended period of time.

Senior Chief and I had to fly into Bahrain again. This time we were close enough for a helo to take us in. We took off in the morning and landed in Bahrain by 1000. We went over to the base CMS vault and picked up our material and headed back to the air field. The helo had to make a stop at Prince Sultan Air Base in Saudi Arabia on the way back to pick up some parts for one of our aircraft. We landed at around 1300. The air base flight line security told us to stay put except for the person who was going to go pick up the parts. They refused to let us off the helo. It was probably 110 degrees out and inside the helo I know the temperature was hitting close to 120 to 130 degrees. We sat there for almost 2 hours while they were searching for those parts we needed. I was becoming nauseated from the heat. Finally the aviation supply guy came back with the parts and we took off. They left the starboard side door open on the helo so we could get some cool air inside once we got a little higher. When we hit about 1,000 feet in altitude it started cooling down immensely. It felt so good. We arrived at the Indy at about 1700 and I was hungry. I hit the officers mess down one deck from my office.

Captain Ellis finally let up on Dave and allowed him to fly around the Gulf a few times after that. I was tired of the flights.

We left the Gulf in November 1990; the ship spent 122 days at sea without a port call. There were only a few privileged people who got off the ship during that time. I happened to be one. I got the privilege to see a part of the world that I never thought I would get a chance to see. Now I can say I have been to that part of the world.

Chapter 8

Morals and Ethics

I love to tell stories about morals and ethics in the Navy. So many sailors, officers and enlisted, do not realize how their morals and ethics affect others around them. You will read stories in this chapter about morals and ethics that maybe you can identify with.

> *A little integrity is better than any career.*
> —Ralph Waldo Emerson

> *The truth of the matter is that you always know the right thing to do. The hard part is doing it.*
> —General H. Norman Schwarzkopf

Use of Deadly Force
By Brian Studnicky

On July 1,1988, the USS Independence CV-62 (Indy) was inport, Norfolk, Virginia. It was holiday routine for the upcoming 4th of July weekend. We had just completed over three weeks of REFTRA (refresher training) of the coast of Guantanamo Bay, Cuba (GITMO for short).

I was on duty that day. At 1050 I was the first one in the chow line on the forward enlisted mess deck. The chow line just happened to be adjacent to the entrance hatch to the Marine Detachment (MARDET). The mess deck didn't open up until 1100 so there was just a short time to wait. The next person to get in line behind me was a sailor whom I had never met but he asked me if this was the chow line, and I told him, "I think it is for today."

The fellow shipmate was RM3 Dion Gaines. While we were waiting in the chow line for ten minutes, I struck up a conversation with the Petty Officer Gaines. On an aircraft carrier (unlike smaller vessels) the ships company consisted of at least 3,000 personnel. You just can't get to know all of them, so there are strangers everywhere.

I was standing forward of the hatch to the MARDET. Gaines was standing aft of the hatch. We were about 6 feet away from each other. There was a sign on the hatch that said "DO NOT ENTER—DEADLY FORCE AUTHORIZED". I was telling Petty Officer Gaines of a story that I heard that 2 weeks ago the Marines apprehended a sailor for not obeying that sign. I pointed the sign out with my index finger expressing my respect to the MARDET's attention to ship security.

Now, there was a video tape camera pointing from the overhead to the hatch with a monitor down in the MARDET's sentry post. On duty down there was CPL Asher Rosinsky. CPL Rosinsky saw me on his monitor and thought that I was obstructing his view by standing too close to the hatch. So he therefore instructed PFC James W. O'Rawe to walk up the ladder and tell me that I must stand clear of the hatch.

As PFC O'Rawe made his way up the ladder, he cracked open the sliding hatch with his pistol out (witnessed by RM3 Gaines) then shut the hatch and went back down the ladder.

CPL Rosinsky asked O'Rawe if he told me to move away, and O'Rawe deceived Rosinsky by lying to him and told him, "Yes, I did."

As I continued to tell my story to Petty Officer Gaines, (having no clue that I was doing anything wrong), I again pointed the sign out again with my index finger. Meanwhile, CPL Rosinsky is viewing his monitor under the impression that I was verbally warned. He was under the impression that I was not only refusing the warning that I never got from PFC O'Rawe, but he interpreted that my index finger on the sign was my middle finger as if I was telling MARDET "fuck you".

CPL Rosinsky ordered 2 Marines to come with him up the ladder. As he whipped open the hatch, he drew out his side arm, placed the barrel up against the right side of my head near my cheekbone and yelled out "WHAT IS YOUR PROBLEM SHIPMATE!!!!!!"

Obviously, as scared as I was I stood there whispering down at him saying "What's wrong?" Rosinsky then yelled, "HIT THE DECK!!!" I hit the deck immediately. They ordered me to spread eagle face down. I tried to ask them what was wrong. Rosinsky yelled, "SHUT UP!" He then asked me what I thought I was doing and accused me of not listening to a verbal warning. I then tried to tell him with my face down in the deck that I didn't do anything wrong. He yelled again, "SHUT UP!" CPL Rosinsky was accompanied by 2 other Marines. One of them was PFC O'Rawe and CPL Tolbert. They properly frisked me and emptied my pockets. When they asked me for my military I. D., I told them it was in my locker (my mistake). They were advising me to carry it with me at all times. I was then handcuffed behind my back and escorted to the master at arms (MAA) shack.

Rosinsky made me put my forehead up against the bulkhead and spread my legs out. He treated me like I was an international terrorist. One of the security patrols working for the MAA thought it was overdone. He saw guns drawn and the way Rosinsky was treating me was uncalled for. I was innocent. I was then uncuffed and spoken to by MAC MacDonald.

I then filled out a report telling everything that happened. I later caught up to Petty Officer Gaines and asked him to repeat to me what he saw. He told me he saw everything and agreed to corroborate my story.

The Indy was only in Norfolk for 6 weeks. We were on our way to our new home port of Naval Air Station North Island in Coronado, California. I had 10 days leave coming to me, so I was going to see my family in Boca Raton, Florida (my hometown). As days went by I took the advice of one of my ship-mates from my division to report this incident to the command master chief, MMCM RICHARD STONE. I immediately did. He took down my information and told me he would speak to Master Sergeant Butler. About 2 days later I found Master Chief Stone in the hanger bay while he was on a survey with the commanding officer of the Indy, Captain William R. "Buzz" Needham. While the CO was engaged in a conversation with another officer, Master Chief Stone called for me to come over. He looked me in the eye and told me my story was all "BULLSHIT". He advised me to talk to Master Sergeant Butler myself. Obviously, the command master chief was not only no help, he was corrupt. I knew for a fact that he never showed up for the ships semi-annual physical readiness test because his fat ass would have failed it easily. So I then phoned Master Sergeant Butler, told him who I was, and then he invited me to sit down with him in his office down in MARDET. He had to assure me that it was safe because I made it clear to him that I was scared to go anywhere near that hatch again.

Anyway, I made it down there and had a lengthy conversation with him. Butler was well aware of Rosinsky's attitude. When I checked on board the Indy, in July 1987, the ship was in Ship's Life Expectancy Program (SLEP) in the Philadelphia Naval Shipyard. The MARDET was not onboard until the tail end of SLEP which was February 1988. The MARDET we received was transferred from the USS Kitty Hawk CV-63. CPL Rosinsky was in that MARDET. He was immediately assigned as Capt. Needham's orderly. The skipper replaced Rosinsky with another Marine, Lance Corporal Pitts because Rosinsky was getting in street fights with sailors on liberty. Most times he got his ass kicked. He came back with a black eye and the skipper said, "You're fired." Rosinsky was only 5'6" 140 pounds at the most. Did he think he could take me? I was 6'4" 245 pounds.

Master Sergeant Butler told me that he would work on Rosinsky's attitude, but that putting a gun to a man's head was standard procedure and that this procedure was approved by the Commandant of the US Marine Corp. WHAT BULLSHIT!

About 2 or 3 weeks after July 1st, the Indy was preparing to go to sea for about 3 days of sea trials. That morning, I was on the forward mess decks buy a soda pop from one of the two soda machines. CPL Rosinsky was buying one at the machine next to mine. He saw me, gently tapped me on my right arm and asked me if we were taking any aircraft with us on this deployment. I stared at him in shock. The nerve he had to confront me with this after what he almost did to me a short time ago. I shook my head and quickly said, "No," and got away from him as soon as I could. Out of hundreds of personnel he could have asked that question to, why me?

About a week later on a Saturday morning, I was on the off-going duty section. I and several other duty personnel had to go ashore to help cast the mooring lines for the USS America CV-66. After that, we were on liberty.

I decided to go have breakfast on the forward mess decks. I grabbed some cereal and sat down at a table. At the next table over CPL Rosinsky sat eating his breakfast with at least 4 of his fellow Marines. As I got up to get milk for my cereal, he got up from his table and I noticed that he was dressed in the same camouflage working uniform he was wearing on July 1st when he could have ended my life with a gun at my head. He was wearing his guard belt carrying a pistol. He confronted me with a smirk on his face and said, "Hey, buddy, did you hear anything yet?" He now obviously knew I was pushing this charge to go to Captain's Mast. I replied and said "No, not yet." Rosinsky then said, "I just hope that you know what you are getting yourself into." I replied, "Same to you." Rosinsky then said, "If you only knew what they are going to do to you." I replied with "I'll be ready." I tried to avoid him as much as I could to protect my case.

I then took my leave to Florida and in my absence, the Executive Officer (XO) Captain Walter Bird conducted an Executive Officer's Investigation (XOI) in his office. He heard only the Marine's point of view and a quote from the MAA. As soon as I got back from leave in Florida, the INDY was about to leave Norfolk, VA for the cruise around the horn to San Diego, CA. Upon my return from leave, I checked to see if I had messages from MAA. I had none.

I then went to the legal office to ask about my case. I met with Lieutenant Commander (LCDR) J. Rolph, the ship's JAG and legal officer. I sat down with the commander and he told me he was very intrigued with my case. However, he, like Capt. Bird, only heard from the Marine's point of view. He was under the impression that I was standing in the chow line and while waiting I was trying to harass the marines purposely standing in front of their hatch and flipping them the bird.

I categorically denied it. LCDR Rolph then looked at me and said, "Oh, would you like to look at the video tape?" I said, "I'd love to look at the video tape. Show me sir." Rolph then said that it wasn't possible at that time. What else would he have said?

LCDR Rolph suggested that I talk to Capt. Bird myself and I did. Capt. Bird was relieved of being the ships XO but was in charge of a tiger team. The Indy was underway for the island of St. Thomas. I went to his office that evening and sat down with him in his stateroom and asked him why CPL Rosinsky didn't go to Captain's Mast or the equivalent of the UCMJ Article 15 non-judicial punishment. Bird chuckled because of the limited amount of information that he had. There was no call for it. I then gave him the untold story. I told him of my eyewitnesses RM3 Gaines and ABH3 Ruggeri. Capt. Bird mentioned to me that my case may be harder to win than I think. Capt. Bird said, "Even though your incident is an inflammatory one, I'll guarantee you that the skipper is going to stick up for his Marines, because they are security to the ship and you are not."
A few days passed on and Capt. Bird then phoned me on the Chief Petty Officer's Mess Deck where I was doing my 90 days of temporary additional duty of mess cooking. I also had to interact with Master Chief Stone and Master Sergeant Butler 3 times a day.

He agreed to re-open the case and let the ship's new XO, Commander Gary B. McEwen decide the disposition.

LCDR Rolph told me when CDR McEwen heard a gun was placed to my head, he was furious. CDR McEwen referred to this assault with a deadly weapon as a very serious charge.

Finally, I knew someone was listening to me. All these meetings were taking place while we were underway sailing the south Atlantic towards the Antarctica Ocean.

The XOI took place with CDR McEwen, Capt. Bird, LCDR Rolph and the MARDET CO Capt. James M. Hille. CPL Rosinsky and I were both ordered in standing before the XO side by side. Rosinsky says, "CPL Rosinsky reporting as ordered, Sir." I started with my story, then Rosinsky told his story. Naturally,

Rosinsky denied my accusations. When I spoke of RM3 Gaines and ABH3 Ruggeri, he wanted them in his office ASAP. They both showed up within 10 minutes time and confirmed my entire story to be the truth. When the XO asked Captain Hille about the video tape that the camera was recording this incident and was in their custody the entire time, he told the XO that the tape was misplaced and couldn't be found. What else was he going to say?

The XO wanted to speak with PFC O'Rawe and CPL Tolbert. He asked O'Rawe about the verbal warning Rosinsky told him to give me. He claimed he gave it, but when Gaines and I both told the XO that he never spoke a word to us. He was then tongue tied.

The XO said that a polygraph would be taken on Rosinsky and that the results would go to the CO. Meanwhile we were heading to Acapulco, then San Diego. One morning on the Chief's mess deck, Master Chief Stone was making some toast and said to me while I was working "Hey, Studnicky. What is going on with that pistol case?" as if he didn't know. I wound up telling him too much. Little did I know at the time that he was good friends with Master Sergeant Butler, and they would do each other favors. I should have realized a while back that Master Chief Stone was not only unsupportive to my case but was working against me. All I was doing was seeking justice. That's all.

So finally, it was November 9, 1988, 4 months and 8 days to the day I could have had my head blown off by waiting in the chow line in port in Norfolk, VA. We were finally going to Captain's Mast.

As I walked into the forecastle (foc'sle), I noticed about a dozen Marines standing in formation. There were also MARDET officers, Capt. Hille, LT Nees, and Master Sergeant Butler.

I stood with my eyewitness Petty Officer Gaines. LCDR Rolph was there. We were all waiting for the skipper to arrive. To my surprise, Master Chief Stone showed up, and I didn't like, then, how this might go. He had a lot of influence on the CO. Also, CPL Rosinsky was asking LCDR Rolph about his witness. He didn't have one at the XOI. So where did this witness come from?

Well, the skipper arrived on the foc'sle and we got started. When the CO approached his lectern, the MAA Master Chief ordered Rosinsky "Hand salute. Two. Uncover. Two." Buzz Needham asked Rosinsky if he understood his rights. Rosinsky replied, "Yes, sir." When Rosinsky was told by the CO to tell his story, he changed it from the story he told at XOI. At XOI Rosinsky stated that he only came out at raised pistol. At this Mast, he told the skipper that because of our size difference he came out of the MARDET compartment, raised his pistol, then took one hand, grabbed my shoulder and pulled me to the ground. Rosinsky was smaller than most women I knew. I was one of the biggest men on the ship.

Capt. Needham's reluctance to ask real questions was making it clear to me that he was not interested in learning the truth but that the truth would hurt the integrity of his Marines if learned. I realized then that Capt. Bird was right. Buzz Needham was biased towards the Marine Detachment. At the XOI even LCDR Rolph said to the XO that obviously someone here was lying.

Then Petty Officer Gaines gave his story. Buzz Needham was coming off on all of us in a nasty way.

Then Captain Hille had a photograph to show the skipper. It was a picture of the hatch to the MARDET with a new sign on it that was inscribed with "DO NOT BLOCK". He wanted the CO to think it was on there on July 1st.

Now, Buzz made himself comfortable by leaning on his lectern and said to me, "Okay, what's your story?" So I gave him my complete story and assured him that the photograph of the new sign that they showed him was not on their hatch the day this happened. Now the skipper was getting angry. At first he believed the gun was placed to my head. Master Chief Stone threw in some input to support MARDET, then out of no where, this dirt bag shows up in coveralls claiming that he was doing work on the forward mess deck and says that he saw me flip the middle finger and that the Marine came out with only a raised pistol. I knew that this was becoming a huge cover up. In the end, the CO ordered Capt. Hille and MARDET to upgrade their means of security to prevent this kind of thing of happening again. He ordered him to get it done that day. He then tried to tell Petty Officer Gaines and myself that we were guilty of putting ourselves in a position where we exposed ourselves to danger. He also tried to state that the drawn gun was so close to us that we both imagined it at my head. Just imagine 2 people imagining the same thing at the same time. Bullshit! So, CPL Rosinsky still got chewed out for drawing the gun. He should have gone to a court martial. Instead, he was dismissed. I was floored. I turned and left the foc'sle. I knew that dirtbag witness and he knew he was lying to cover this up had eye contact with me.

I returned to my work center, the Chief's mess deck, and got a message that LCDR Rolph wanted to see me. I went to his office and sat down with him. He knew I was upset at the outcome of mast. He wanted me to know that he believed my story to be the truth. He told me that Rosinsky passed the so called polygraph test but I was never privileged to the questions he was asked. I then again returned to the chief's mess deck when lunch was starting.

Master Chief Stone came down and while I was on the floor cleaning up tables, he started to harass me by giving me petty orders like change the channel on the TV, clean up this and clean up that.

We arrived at North Island Naval Air Station on October 8, 1988. About two weeks went by and I was headed back to the Indy from liberty. It was about 2100. I was on the base and walking towards the ship about 2 blocks away. As I approached the street corner, I saw about 3 Marines in their working uniforms approaching the corner. We were about to cross paths. I could hear the one Marine from a distance, but as dark as it was I couldn't identify any of them. Once we were all under the street light I could clearly identify CPL Asher Rosinsky as well as he did me. Rosinsky then yelled out, "THAT'S HIM!! THERE; HE IS RIGHT THERE!!!" Obviously, his conversation was about me. I kept looking at him as he and the other jarheads were looking at me. Rosinsky then stomped his boot at me to try to scare me or make more trouble. He was well known for that throughout the ship. I just kept walking.

The biggest joke of it all was a month later when CPL Rosinsky confronted me on liberty on the base and challenged me to a fight off base. I declined his request. Rosinsky was eventually transferred to Camp Pendleton, and I never heard from him again.

My End of Active Obligated Service (EAOS) was not until January 11, 1991, but that day, November 9, 1988, left a large impact on my decision to leave the Navy when my time was up. I trusted my leaders to do what they knew was morally right, and they turned their backs on me.

Capt. Needham was finally relieved of command of the Indy and was transferred to Pearl Harbor, Hawaii. He became the first Needham in his family history to not make admiral.

The new CO Capt. Tom Slater transferred Master Chief Stone off the Indy. He knew he was trash.

Note from the Editor: Impugn means to assail by words or arguments or oppose or attack as false or lacking integrity. Mr. Studnicky may be impugning the motives of others and that is okay. If the actions taken against him were not honest and lacking integrity, he has all the right in the world to speak his mind. Speaking your mind is none other than your opinion. The First Amendment gives us that right. I have allowed Brian to speak his opinion and it is a story I felt needed to be told. I was stationed on the Indy for part of the time that Brian Studnicky was on board and can vouch for the types of actions that some of the officers took. I knew some of them as an assistant department head because I had to fill in from time to time as the acting department head and eventually took over as department head. This story tells about one sailor's troubles. There are situations just like this that have occurred in the Navy. This story shows how lies and power corrupt those that you should be able to trust. In my last book, "It Wasn't Just A Job; It Was An Adventure," I had several stories about senior officers that used their power and authority to do whatever they felt like doing and if you confronted them on their immoral acts, they would try to destroy your career through bad fitness reports or performance evaluations. I will not pull any punches with anyone who is morally and ethically corrupt. I thank Brian for sharing his experience on the Indy.......Donald Johnson

Traitors and Polygraphs
By Donald Johnson

In 1985 retired Chief Warrant Officer John Walker, a former enlisted radioman, was arrested for espionage and spying for the Russians. He had enlisted the help of his brother who retired as a Lieutenant Commander in the submarine services, his son, an operations yeoman on board an aircraft carrier and his best friend, Jerry Whitworth, a senior chief radioman. He even tried recruiting his daughter who was in intelligence in the Army. He never thought he would get caught. His alcoholic wife knew what he was doing and she had told people about him, but she was not to be believed because of her alcoholism.

After the spy ring was uncovered and all concerned were arrested, the Navy began to find out how this could have happened. I was livid that an American sailor would turn on his own country for money and prestige. If the federal government had put me in the same cell with him, I probably would have killed him and saved the government the expense of caring for him for the rest of his life. I was madder at John Walker than the rest of his cohorts. John Walker had a way with words and was able to convince the rest of them to follow through with what he wanted.

The Navy began to do background investigation updates on a routine basis after that. I had had a clearance since coming back into the Navy in 1976 and never had an update done. Many others that I knew had had a clearance for 20 years with no update. That changed with the Walker case.

I had to fill out paper work on every duty station and address I had lived at for the past ten years, 1976-1986. There were investigators out questioning my neighbors, friends, relatives, and co-workers. Then it was time for a polygraph. That did not bother me until......

I was scheduled for a polygraph during one of the in port periods before the ship was scheduled to deploy overseas in early 1987. I was due to transfer in January 1987 to an officer in charge billet at Mare Island. I know they were going to scrutinize me because of that billet.

On the day of the polygraph, I hopped out of bed, had breakfast, got my guys off to work and checked my message traffic before I left. I really had no problem with polygraph because I had nothing to hide. Or at least I didn't think so.

When I got to the Naval Investigative Service Office off 32nd Street in San Diego, I was briefed on what I was going to be asked. I was asked questions like: Have you ever stolen anything from the Navy? Have you ever cheated on an exam? Have you ever thought about selling secrets to a foreign government? Have you ever compromised shipboard security by destroying classified keying material early and lying about the destruction? Have you ever lied to your chain of command?

As we started going over the questions, they wanted me to answer the questions truthfully before they started the polygraph. And then they began asking me the questions before hooking me up to the polygraph.

Have you ever stolen anything from the Navy including pens, paper pads, tools, etc.? I thought about it and wondered about the 2 or 3 dozen Navy pens I had at home. I always carried a pen in my shirt pocket and when I would go home, take it out and forget to put it in my pocket the next day. Would that be considered stealing? I ask them that. They told me it could be, but probably not. So they decided to rephrase the question. **Have you ever stolen anything from the Navy other than what we discussed here today?** I would answer, no.

Have you ever cheated on an exam? I told them, no. However, when the hooked me up for the polygraph, I began thinking about this question. And when they got to this question, I had to stop and ask them a question. I had told them that they had juggled my brain a little bit and I would have to say that I did cheat on an exam if that is what you call it. I had taken several Navy Correspondence Courses and at that time the answer sheets were the type that you had to scratch off the answers, like the scratch and win lottery tickets. I had found out from a friend that if you take a pen light, you could shine in on the back of the answer sheets and see the answers. I completed about six courses that way and sent them in to be graded. I always missed a few on purpose so that it looked like I did not cheat. Those correspondence courses may have helped me get selected and promoted through the Navy's LDO program. So they rephrased the question. **Have you ever cheated on an exam other than the times that you told us about?** I then answered, no, and this time it was the truth.

Have you ever thought about selling secrets to a foreign government? I told them, no.

Have your ever compromised shipboard security by destroying classified keying material early and lying about the destruction? I told them that I had destroyed classified keying material early once and that the CMS Custodian wanted me to lie by signing the destruction form that it was destroyed as scheduled. I refused to sign the destruction form. I gave them the name of the CMS Custodian who asked me to do that. The problem with destroying CMS material early is that if there was a need for the keying material for a special operation, then one unit would be without the material so they would have to supersede that material and go to the next set. When I inadvertently destroyed that material, the CMS Custodian was going to have to send out a message placing us on report for doing so. He did not want to do that and get the CO in trouble as well. A security violation would have negated any qualifications to win the coveted squadron Communications Green C award, a part of the squadron Battle Efficiency competition. That forgery got that ship a Green C award that year. NIS had that information. They wanted to know why I did not report the violation. I told them I did not want to receive an adverse evaluation.

Have you ever lied to your chain of command? I told them, no, but then during the questioning while hooked up to the polygraph, I began thinking about this question. They stopped the polygraph when I asked them to. I told them that I would lie to the chain of command to protect my men. I gave them an instance of where we received a communications exercise message via our broadcast one Sunday while we were at anchor at Seal Beach off loading ammunition before going north for overhaul in Bremerton Navy Shipyard. We had a TV set up to watch the Super Bowl. While we were watching TV in radio we did not notice that the broadcast printer had run out of paper. When one of my radiomen noticed that, he changed the paper and the first message that popped out was this exercise message. We had five minutes to get a receipt from a Naval Communications Station who would relay the message to the National Command Center in Washington. Our response was 3 minutes from the time the message was printed out. I looked at the system receipt time. That printer had been off about 20 minutes. I was wondering how I was going to send out an after action report and how I was going to word it without my radiomen getting in trouble because of my allowing them to watch the Super Bowl at anchor. I came up with a good answer and then took the message up to the CO for signature. Charlie Barker, the CO, had been a radioman in his early days of the Navy and knew how we operated. When he saw my response, he questioned me at length and then signed it. As I was walking out, he told me that was a pretty good lie. Don't let it happen again. I was startled. I never lied to Charlie ever again. I told the NIS agents a few other things that I had lied about and got away with it. They wrote those down and then we went back to questioning and they rephrased that question the same as the others.

When it was all over, the head NIS agent in charge of the polygraphs told me that he knew I was not a spy, but he felt I was not entirely truthful on many of the other personal integrity questions. I told him that he got me to thinking about all of those questions and about how the Navy causes you to lie in order to protect yourself. He told me that he was glad that I came clean with all of them in the end. I then professed to never lie again and if it caused me to get a bad fitness report, so be it.

Not Recommended for Re-enlistment
By Donald Johnson

I reported onboard USS Independence (CV-62) in January 1990. The Indy was beginning to go through workups and begin the training exercises that would lead up to refresher training before deploying to the Western Pacific and Indian Ocean in June 1990. The admin officer had tried to set up my reporting interview with the commanding officer, Captain Tom Slater, several times over the first six weeks.

Finally, during the sixth week during some training flight exercises of qualifying pilots carrier take off and landings (carrier quals), we got to meet. One late night we had a bump and crunch accident on the flight deck that caused damage to two aircraft. The CO had to get word to the Commander, Naval Air Forces, Pacific, at North Island Naval Air Station in San Diego. We were in an area of the Pacific operating area where communication with the outside world is almost impossible. My radiomen were trying their best to attempt to get communications up so that the CO could get his reports out.

I had no knowledge of this happening because I slept through the night. My radiomen went to tell my boss what was going on and he went back to sleep. At first light one of my chiefs was up on the signal bridge and saw a sailor using a cell phone. Back in those days, the cell phone was the size of a small two way radio. He was talking to his wife. The chief asked the sailor if he could take the phone down to the CO and let him call COMNAVAIRPAC. He was able to call them and make his report.

When I awoke that morning, I did my morning duties of shaving, showering and going to breakfast. I then went up to radio to get my message traffic and that is when I found out about the comm problems. They had just re-established comms with everyone. I felt it was my duty to report to the CO on all the problems and let him know that we had just re-established comms with the outside world. I had no idea that my chief had taken that sailor's cell phone down to the CO to use.

I began calling around to find out where the CO was located. I found that he was in the Operations office. I went down there. He was talking to the Operations Officer, Captain Bunnell. There were two other officers and a few enlisted sailors in the office. When I introduced myself to the CO, Captain Slater, he went off on me, yelling about how screwed up Communications Department was. As he was screaming at me I tried breaking in so I could get my side of the story in. He told me to shut up and not interrupt him and once he is through chewing on me, if he wants me to say something he will let me. When he was through chewing on me, he left.

I asked Captain Bunnell if the CO was like that all the time. He said he was a screamer and the best thing to do is to let him scream and get it out of his system. Captain Bunnell told me that he would call down later and probably ask me to lunch in his inport cabin. Two hours later Captain Slater called down to radio to invite my boss, Lieutenant Commander Jack Powers and myself to lunch.

At lunch, Captain Slater apologized for his screaming episode and for his put down of my radiomen. He also told me that I had big pair of testicles for trying to break in on his tirade. He told me that I handled it better than any officer that he had chewed out. I accepted that as something that would be good for me and that he would probably never do that again to me. And he never did. We both then had a little respect for each other's positions. He then told me about the cell phone which my chief had still not told me about because he had gone down to the CPO quarters to sleep since he was up all night trying to get comms. Captain Slater then ordered Jack and I to get a cell phone system installed onboard so that if we had problems in the future that we would be able to make those emergency calls.

After that incident, Captain Slater backed me on all my decisions which I really felt good about. One incident that he backed me on was not allowing one of my radiomen to re-enlist.

I had an RM3 that wanted to re-enlist. He was one of those troublemakers that got shipped off to a TAD assignment—the tool room. I also found out that I had about a dozen radiomen who were farmed out all over the ship, places like mess cooking, side cleaners, tool room, Special Services, etc.

Once I found out where all my TAD people were and I wanted to know what kind of sailors they were. I told all my Chiefs that we don't send out dirt bags TAD until we either get them up to par with what the Navy expects of them or kick them out of the Navy. I told them that we will keep our problem children in house. I did not want to air my dirty laundry outside the department.

The tool room RM3 was immediately re-assigned to CR division and was immediately placed on a watch schedule to find out what type of radioman that he was. I also found out that he was married to a DT3 (Dental Tech). It was an interracial marriage.

After three months, performance evaluations were due. I took all the negative inputs from his three months in CR and his nine months in the tool room and put together a negative eval on him which had to be signed by the CO. My input on the evaluation for re-enlistment was "Not Recommended for Re-Enlistment". Slater signed the eval and so did this RM3.

Three months later this RM3 put a request in to re-enlist for four years so he could transfer with his wife to Key West. The department Leading Chief Petty Officer was Signalman Master Chief Comstock. He received this RM3's request to re-enlist knowing that we had not recommended him for re-enlistment. Master Chief Comstock had argued with my Senior Chief over his recommendation to approve his request to re-enlist. The Senior Chief I believe wanted to just rid the ship of this non-productive sailor and let some other command deal with him. Master Chief Comstock wanted to just let him finish his enlistment and then he could move with his wife to Key West.

I had my Senior Chief and Master Chief Comstock come in and sit with me and discuss this request. I told the Senior Chief that if we recommended in a person's performance evaluation that they were "Not Recommended for Re-enlistment" that was what it meant unless the sailor did a 180 degree turn around. This guy was still unproductive and causing problems. I asked the Senior Chief if he wanted to go up and explain to the Executive Officer (XO), Captain Bixler and the CO why he recommended him for re-enlistment and everyone else up the chain recommended disapproval of the request. Senior Chief pulled the request back and had the RM3 re-submit. The request was disapproved all the way up the chain including the XO and CO. I had to go brief both on the sailor and how he was such a troublemaker who would do the minimum to stay out of trouble. Both agreed with me based on the last evaluation.

The request went back to the RM3 who got mad and turned in a request to see the CO. I said no problem with that request. I forwarded the request to the XO. We talked for quite some time about how this could ruin this young man's life. I told the XO that if we went into battle that I did not want this man in battle with me, because I would not be able to trust him or depend on him. That sold the XO.

The request then went to the CO. Captain Slater and I both talked about this sailor again and at length. This was on a Thursday afternoon. The CO was going to hold Captain's Mast the next morning before we arrived in port North Island. He told me that he wanted to see this RM3 the next morning at 0700 on the starboard bridge wing as his first mast case. The RM3 wanted a closed mast. The CO ordered an open mast with witnesses from both sides.

I ordered the Senior Chief to contact the RM3 about this 7am mast. No one could find this guy. We were at sea. At 0300 this guy came into berthing and was told to be ready at 0630 because he was going to see the CO. To this day no one knows where this guy was hiding out on the ship. He was told to get a hold of his witnesses and that they had to be there at 0700. I had already contacted witnesses for my side of the argument which included the officer and chief in charge of the tool room.

The RM3 showed up at 0630 outside the bridge wing. I knew that I had nothing to worry about because of the way he was dressed. He had on a wrinkled dress blue jumper with no neckerchief, pants that were not obviously his because they were too long and were tight around his waist, unshined boondockers (not dress shoes), and a dirty white hat.

At 0700 sharp the Chief Master at Arms (MAC) had the RM3 enter the bridge wing and stand at attention. When Slater came in, the MAC had the RM3 uncover. Captain Slater continued on over to the window and put his coffee cup down and then came back over to the lectern and looked at the RM3. He said something like this:

"RM3 (so and so), I understand you want to talk to me." RM3 says, "Yes, sir." Slater says, "I understand that you want to re-enlist in my Navy." RM3 says, "Yes, sir."

At this time, Slater becomes the screamer that he is known as and begins a tirade yelling at the RM3. "YOU WANT TO RE-ENLIST IN MY NAVY LOOK-ING LIKE THAT? RM3 (so and so), YOU ARE NOT GOOD ENOUGH TO RE-ENLIST IN MY NAVY!"

At this time he quieted down a little and asked him a couple of questions as to why he wanted to re-enlist. The RM3 then reiterated about his wife receiving orders to Key West and that he wanted to go there with her.

Captain Slater then began looking over everyone that was there as witnesses for or against this guy. He said, "I see that you brought some witnesses or character witnesses. LT Johnson also has character witnesses. I WANT TO KNOW IF THERE IS ANYONE IN THIS BRIDGE WING RIGHT NOW WHO THINKS THIS SCUMBAG IS GOOD ENOUGH TO RE-ENLIST IN MY NAVY." No one spoke up, not even the RM3's buddies. Slater told the RM3 that he would reconsider re-enlistment if he would turn his performance around over the next six months when his enlistment is up. If he could show that he could perform up to par in the Navy. Captain Slater then turned to the RM3 and told him he was dismissed. The RM3 spoke up to try to tell him something else and Captain Slater yelled at him and told him to get the hell off his bridge.

This RM3 did not get along with anyone. His performance stayed the same. He then got his wife involved in his quest to re-enlist. His wife then started calling me and whining to me about us not allowing him to re-enlist. I told her that he was not a good sailor. He may seem like a good sailor to her because she was married to him, but he was not doing his job on this ship. I told her that if he couldn't do his job properly on board this ship that he probably would not be able to do a good job in Key West. I told her that he can get out and follow her to Key West. She said that they would lose an entire paycheck. I told her that if he was as good a sailor as she thought he was, that he could probably get a good job in Key West working at the base exchange or commissary. She got nasty with me and called me all types of names that I could have brought her up on charges under the UCMJ, but I decided against that since her emotions were running her life at that time. She threatened to bring racial discrimination charges against me. I told her to bring them on. I did not hear any more from her and he eventually got out of the Navy. To this day, I don't remember the sailor's name.

Where is Your ID Card?
By Donald Johnson

As a senior petty officer and later a commissioned officer, I had young sailors that would try to get away with anything that they could just like I used to. I used a lot of stories and I heard a lot of stories.

While on USS Independence (CV-62) I had 90 radiomen and 12 signalmen. I could write a whole book on excuses alone from the stories I got off these men; however, one story I love to tell is about a young radioman by the name of Young. He was an RM3, radioman third class petty officer. He already had a record when I got on board. He had gone to Captain's Mast for a fight he had with a shipmate on the mess decks when he was mess cooking. I guess he was getting beat in the fight so he grabbed a knife to protect himself and was brought up on those charges. He stayed clean for a while and was promoted to RM3 right after I reported on board.

We had already returned from Operation Desert Shield and was going through a mini-overhaul pier side in North Island to prepare for the turnover with the USS Midway (CV-41). The ships were swapping homeports with the Indy going to Yokosuka, Japan and the Midway going to San Diego to be decommissioned.

In April or May of 1991, many of my men were beginning to go on leave to be with loved ones and friends before we departed in June for Pearl Harbor to accomplish the turnover. RM3 Young was one of those that took a 30 day leave.

When he did not return from leave on his scheduled day of return, we got concerned and my RMC called his home and found that he was home and was afraid to return to the ship without his ID card. He had told the Chief that he had left it at a restaurant in Alameda when he and a few of his friends departed from up there. I told the Chief to call him back and tell him to report to the ship immediately and that we would replace his lost ID card. If he refused to report, then he would be placed on report.

When the Chief called him back, his mother answered the phone and she told the Chief that Young had left to go get his ID card. The Chief relayed my message plus his own that if he did not report by Monday morning when the ship got underway for sea trials that he would miss ship's movement that was more serious than being on an unauthorized absence. I wished that he would not have told him that. He was already in trouble and he knew it.

Young showed up on Monday morning with his ID card in hand. I told the Chief to write him up for a five day unauthorized absence and begin his investigation as to what happened. When I received the Chief's report, I knew that Young was lying. I was tired of the lies and deceptions, so I had the Chief bring Young in to see me. I had the Master Chief Radioman, RMCM DeGuzman, in as a witness to the questioning.

When Young came in, I had him stand at attention with both the RMC and RMCM there. I began questioning Young on all types of things. First I asked him why he did not come back and get his ID card replaced. He told me that he was afraid that we would keep him restricted to the ship for ten days until he received a new ID card. I asked him if he knew that he was in trouble for not returning to the ship on the day he was supposed to. He said that he tried to get an extension of leave. I told him that I told the Chief that I was denying that and he was to return to the ship.

I then tried some deception of my own. I knew northern California pretty well since I had just came from there and because my family was still in Suisun City near Travis Air Force Base. I drove home every chance that I got. I began to question him about his travels in northern California. I asked him what restaurant he had left his ID card at. He told me that it was at Denny's in Alameda. When I asked him which Denny's, he looked puzzled, so I helped him. I said was it the Denny's on Webster at the Motel 6 or was it the one on Hegenberger Road. He still looked puzzled, so I described both places a little more and he told me it was the Denny's on Webster. I asked Young who found and held his ID for him. He told me that the restaurant manager did.

Now it was time for a little more deception. I then told Young that I would stop by Denny's on my way home that weekend and talk with the manager of the restaurant and if his story was true I would more than likely drop the charges and give him some EMI (extra military instruction). If he was lying, I would make sure that he received the harshest punishment for his infraction. I told him that I was from northern California and knew where many of the cheap eating places were in all of the military towns up north. I then dismissed him.

An hour later the Chief came in and told me that Young was scared to death. He told the Chief that he had lied about the ID card because he wanted a few extra days off. I then pushed his offense report through to the XO for XO Investigation. I was so mad at Young and wanted him punished for lying and taking advantage of the people who would take care of him if he was honest. The XO let him off with some EMI only because I had several men go to Captain's Mast for various offenses. The XO did not want to bring more attention to my department. The department was beginning to turn around because of my hard as nails leadership something that was needed to make the radiomen begin to shape up. I also had a racial discrimination complaint filed against me by a group of African American radiomen. The allegations were unfounded after a lengthy investigation. What was found was a lot of favoritism in the African American ranks in my department. That was when I decided to clamp down on those who wanted to buck the system. The XO did not want it to look like I was getting retribution by punishing the African Americans. I did not agree, but what could I do. I let it go. I knew that what went around would come around for Young. It did after I retired. Young missed ship's movement out of Subic the same day I left the ship to fly back to the U.S. to retire.

Decisions, Decisions
By Donald Johnson
Copyright © 1997

This is a speech that I gave at my Toastmasters club in September 1997.

"When faced with a decision—decide. When faced with a choice—choose. Sitting on the fence will leave you tense because you neither win nor lose!"
This is a quote by Barry Spilchuk.

How many of you are in some type of management or leadership role at work and have to make decisions from time to time?

How many of you hate to make decisions?

Well, Mr. Toastmaster, fellow Toastmasters and most welcome guests.

I am here to tell you that if I worked for you, I would have your job in six months.

You are probably asking yourself right now how that might happen.

I will give you a couple of examples in my Navy career where that happened and how I was elevated into my bosses' positions because of their failure to make a decision or failure to act on a situation that could have caused injury or death or loss of classified information.

The first example comes from the USS Belleau Wood (LHA-3). I was the Radio Officer and Assistant Communications Officer. My boss, the Communications Officer, was Lieutenant Commander (LCDR) Jim Dunlap. Jim was previously enlisted, an electronics technician. He received a commission upon completing his college degree and was assigned to flight school where he qualified for piloting the P-3 Orion sub hunter. It was a four engine propeller driven aircraft. He was an outstanding pilot. Jim was single and not a bad leader, but he had his little idiosyncrasies. This guy was into passing gas wherever he was and did not care where he was. I did not like that part of him. He also was a meddler.

The Belleau Wood had just returned to San Diego from our Western Pacific and Indian Ocean deployment. We were on a stand down for the holidays. Our amphibious squadron commander wanted to give us an administrative inspection before we went to the shipyard in Bremerton, Washington for an overhaul. One part of this inspection was checking our procedures in storing nuclear control orders (NCO). I was one part of a two man team and Andy, the CMS custodian was one part of another two man team. Jim was the over all coordinator. Jim had put off a lot of things dealing with this inspection. I know that if he had prepared a little more that he would not have gotten in trouble.

He controlled all shipboard safe combinations including the combinations to the NCO safes. These safes were actually two safes in one. There was a smaller inner safe. So there were two combinations to each safe. Team member number one had the combination to the outer safe and team member number two had the combination to the inner safe. The combinations had to be placed in special envelopes and placed in separate safes away from the NCO safes.

One evening when I was getting ready to leave the ship to go home, Jim came into my office and gave me several safe combination envelopes to put in my office safe. I did not ask him anything. I just assumed they were combinations to all of the stateroom safes that he was trying to update. I opened my safe and tossed them in. I then went home for the evening.

The next morning the inspection began. Everything in my part of the inspection went well. Then it was time for the NCO inspection. The squadron Communications Officer and Jim did not get along and he wanted so badly to find something on Jim. Everything appeared to be okay until they got to the combinations. When Jim told him that he stored all of the combinations in my safe, the squadron CommO jumped for joy. He had finally caught Jim in the middle of a major security violation. The CO and XO were informed. They both came up to my office to find out what happened. We all did not feel that there was a security violation because I had not opened the safe since I tossed the envelopes in there.

The CO convinced the squadron commander of that, too. But Jim was not in good favor with the CO. The CO felt that Jim could have done a better job at managing the NCO accounts and that he made a bad decision. Jim was livid at the squadron CommO. He was also not too happy with me in not catching that mistake. Oh, well! The world keeps on going.

When we arrived at the shipyard in Bremerton, Washington for an overhaul, I was made a departmental overhaul coordinator. I soon had my overhaul schedule pretty much set in stone. I had my teams all set and made sure that they did what they were supposed to be doing each day. I had weekly meetings to find out how much they had completed on each job. Jack liked to interfere in work schedules. When I was off the ship, he would get the teams to stop what they were doing and start other projects that were not scheduled to start for a week or two. He and I argued over that a few times. He was causing my teams to get behind. I went to the CO and he told me to just hang in there.

Jim went on leave and while he was on leave, the CO received a call from the Chief of Naval Personnel, Admiral Boorda, who was looking for a candidate to go to the Marine Corps Staff and Command College in Quantico, Virginia. The CO told him that he had just the candidate, Jim Dunlap. When Jim got back from leave he found out that he was going and tried to get out of it. The CO told him that he could not. Jim had about two weeks before he left. Jim was making bad decisions. I am glad the CO helped in the transfer.

Jim left and that left the department to Andy and me. We were co-department heads. Everyone knew who actually ran the department.

When I transferred to the Independence in 1990, I was informed by the guy I was replacing that the CommO was being scrutinized and was about to be fired as the department head and that I may end up with the job. I did not like the sound of that. I did not talk to my new boss, LCDR Jack Powers until they day I reported.

Jack and I sat down and talked pretty much all day long. He was carrying a walkie talkie or two-way radio that was the size and weight of a large brick. That is what we called those things, bricks. Each department head had one and when Gun Train called you, you went running to find out what the CO wanted. Jack was so scared of the CO. Every time I heard "CommO, Gun Train," Jack's legs would turn to Jell-O and would go flying out the door. He would some times trip over the knee knockers and drop his radio.

The XO had told me not to do Jack's job, just mentor him and tell him what he needed to do to do his job. The CO told me the same thing. I tried each and every day to tell him what he needed to do. I felt sorry for the guy. He was once a C-2 COD (carrier onboard delivery or passenger/cargo plane) pilot and he had a brain aneurism, which grounded him from ever flying again. He had a steel plate in his head. He had a beautiful wife and six kids. The brain damage, I feel, caused him to lose some of his decision making skills. He was disorganized and some times disoriented.

There were two things that got him fired. I had addressed one item to him several times and the other one just a couple of times and Dave Rausch, my CMS custodian addressed the second item to him a couple of times as well.

I developed the ship's underway communication plans with my chiefs a week before we would get underway each time. I had told all of them including Jack that under no circumstances would any changes be made after Friday's at 1700. I normally drove home to my northern California home on the weekends before getting underway.

This particular underway time was one of the first times out to sea since under going a mini-overhaul pier side before heading to Japan for home port change. We were going out to sea for some carrier quals including helicopters.

I had the comm plan in place when I left on this Friday afternoon. I got in on Sunday evening and went up to Radio to make sure the comm plan was set in place. The radiomen told me that it was.

The next morning when we got underway we could not talk to any of the helicopters that were flying around wanting to land. We could not talk with them even though the radios were working good. I had gone up to the UHF transceivers room to make sure everything was set up properly and the Chief was there. The Chief was a new chief and was being tested. I asked him 20 questions and he answered me back. Then I began looking at the comm plan and noticed that it was a modified comm plan. The original was sitting next to it. I asked the Chief if he had changed the comm plan and he told me that he had. I asked him if he had sent out a change to the comm plan and he told me that Jack was going to take care of that. Jack never did. I immediately told the Chief to go back to the original comm plan so we could contact the aircraft. Once he shifted the frequencies to the ones on the original comm plan, we were then able to talk to the helos trying to land.

I then went down to Radio to find Jack and asked him why he did not call me on the comm plan and that they had made some changes. He said he did not feel I needed to be bothered. I then asked him if he had sent out a change to the comm plan so all the aircraft squadrons got the new frequencies. He looked at me puzzled. I asked him how he thought the aircraft were going to talk to us on the new frequencies if they did not know what they were. He just shrugged his shoulders.

I then left to go up to the bridge to tell the CO what had happened. The CO was madder than a hornet. At the end of our conversation, Dave Rausch came up to the bridge to tell the CO that everything was going well on his CMS inspection. The CO turned around with a puzzled look this time. He said what inspection. Dave said that he had scheduled a CMS inspection for this at sea period so we could get it out of the way before we left for Japan. The CO said that he was not informed of the inspection and that he should know of any inspectors who come on board his ship. Dave said that he told Jack and he assumed that Jack would tell you. I then spoke up and told the CO that I had reminded Jack three times to tell him. Jack never did. I told the CO that I should have told him. The CO said that was not my job. It was Jack's responsibility. The CO dismissed both of us. As I was headed down to Radio, I stopped in the Operations office. I heard the Ops bosses two-way radio spouting out, "CommO, Gun Train. Lay to bridge immediately." The Ops boss wanted to know what it was all about and I told him. The Ops boss then told me that Jack would be fired now.

The CO called me to his at sea cabin an hour later and told me that I was now his Communications Officer until he could get someone in to replace Jack. Jack packed his stuff and was gone on the COD that evening. I never saw him again.

Bad decisions, no decision or wishy washy decisions can get you fired or at least transferred early to a place that you don't want to go. So if you don't want to get fired or laid off due to shoddy decision making, ensure you make the best decision. Work with those people who know their job the best and use them to make you and your team look good. Give credit where credit is due. You will undoubtedly make the right decision.

What is leadership anyway?

Bobby Biehl states that Leadership is knowing what to do next..... knowing why it's important..... knowing how to bring appropriate resources to bear on the need at hand.

Knowing what to do next…fits in with the leaders vision…This person knows where he wants to go and how to get there (in most cases).

Knowing why it's important…also fits in with the leaders vision…This person knows why it is important to get where you are going…your groups goal.

Knowing how to bring appropriate resources to bear on the need at hand…This person knows where to find the resources to get the job done to reach your goal. Some times it is people. Some times you will have to persuade the people to lend a hand in reaching this goal.

So know what to do next, know why it is important and know how to obtain the resources you need to get the job done.

I tried my best to be a mentor to both of these officers and get them to make the right decisions. I just happened to have two COs who had some faith in me to pick up the pieces and fix the problems. I did in each case.

I will never forget the leadership of those two COs. I learned from them. It is my wishes for each of you to find someone in your work environment to be your mentor. Listen to them. Maybe it won't be so hard to make that decision.

More Indy Stories
By Brian Studnicky and Donald Johnson

The following are several short stories that came out of e-mail chats that Brian and I had. He brought back a lot of memories and most of them were not good ones. As the stories are put together I will include Brian's story first with mine following on what I knew about the incidents or about a similar incident.

Chief Postal Clerk's Death

Brian:

Were you on board when the postal chief hung himself in the ship's post office? It happened in early 1990. The postal chief had a DUI in San Diego that night. The cops brought him to base security and then base security took him to ship's security. They let him go to the Chiefs mess deck. It was about midnight. He had a few cups of coffee. Security thought we was o.k. to go to his rack. He was so down and ashamed. He went to his ships post office, made a noose and hung himself. One of his clerks came by the office that night, called a medical emergency, but it was too late. He had already died.

Slater (CO) had quarters on the flight deck that following Monday morning. Normally, he would order us all to stand at ease. This time he made us all stand at attention and announced the bad news to the entire ships company. He then urged all department heads to have lengthy talks with all personnel to prevent it from happening again. Boy, do I remember that week.

Donald:

I remember the Postal Chief incident. I was fairly new on board and still trying to find my way around. When I heard about the hanging, I began to wonder why he did that. My chiefs kept me pretty much informed to what went on in the Goat Locker. They told me that this chief had been arrested for DUI two other times and that this chief had been through alcohol rehab. This was his last hoorah which meant that he would not only be prosecuted by the civilian authorities and end up going to jail for while, but the Navy would begin the administrative discharge process and boot him out. He did not have enough time to retire. This was probably on his mind when he committed suicide.

Screaming COs

Donald: (Part of this story was told in an earlier story. I am including it here to segue into Brian's story.

I didn't do so well on the Indy either. I reported onboard in Jan 90. All officers have to check in with the CO within a week after reporting aboard. I did not meet Slater until six weeks onboard. The admin officer kept postponing my check-in.

Six weeks after reporting aboard we were conducting ops and carrier quals off San Diego. My radiomen had lots of problems one night and could not communicate with anyone ashore. We had a bump and scrunch on the flight deck with a couple of aircraft, both F-14s.

The CO and Ops boss had to get a message to North Island and a couple of other commands and could not. My radiomen never came down to wake me to let me know. My boss knew about the problem, but failed to let me know.

When I got up and went to the radio shack, I found out what had happened. They had just got comms back when I got up there. I decided I had better go see Slater and let him know what was going on. I found him in the Ops office. He ripped into me like it was my fault that my guys could not get his message out. It wasn't the fault of my guys either. That was when I found out that Slater was a screamer. I tried to interrupt him twice while he was chewing away and he finally told me to shut up and if he wanted me to say anything, he would allow it when he was through chewing my backside. He did not allow me to say anything.

Ellis was a total opposite. He would chew on you and you wouldn't know it until you left his cabin. You would stop a few feet out of his cabin and say, "He just chewed me out, didn't he?"

Slater didn't make admiral; Ellis did.

Brian:

WOW! That was an awful experience. I only saw Slater chew out a first class on captain's call. He was a work center supervisor who didn't agree with the courtesy turnover in the event a sailor from his division came back to the ship drunk and disorderly. The Master at Arms would set up mattresses on the forward mess decks and let them sleep there rather than interrupt their shipmates in the berthing.

The first class was from engineering. He sent a letter to Slater questioning why a supervisor (E-6) or above had to escort him from the enlisted brow to the mess decks. Well, Slater revealed his name, balled him out viciously on the air with the rest of the crew watching and lectured him on being responsible for the men in his division.

You see, Buzz Needham didn't have the wherewithal to compliment the Engineering Department largely due to the fact that he was an aviator (Airedale).
That alone created a morale problem and the Engineering Department hated Buzz for that. The snipes hated us Airedales in return for that.

So Slater had the burden of making up to Engineering something that Buzz Needham didn't know how to do. So Slater sucked up to Engineering every chance he got, but on that morning of Captains Call he told Petty Officer (so and so), "You've been doing a great job down there in Engineering and I've complimented you since you came on board, but this time your going to get a god dammit".

A good friend of mine also witnessed in the Primary Flight (PriFly) Control Tower where the Air Boss sits, Slater was sitting up there for a sea trial the week before he took command. Needham came up to PriFly to chew out the Air Boss. Slater then stepped in and chewed out Needham knowing Needham was still the skipper.

So I can certainly believe your story.

Gundecking

Brian:

Subject: Gundecking

I'm sure you remember that title. *(Note: Gundecking is a term for signing off on completed preventive maintenance without actually doing the maintenance.)*

In 1987 Buzz Needham made an example out of a work center supervisor stressing the importance of Preventive Maintenance System (PMS). When he found out about any gundecking and who was responsible, he held Captain's Mast live in the ships TV studio. At 13:50 there was an announcement on the 1mc (general announcing system). "There will be a Captain's Mast on site TV. All hands not actually on watch are encouraged to view this presentation." I had only been in the navy for a year, but what a lesson we were about to learn.

Needham was furious. Two sailors were charged, a first class petty officer and a fireman (E-3). He started with the first class and ripped him to shreds. His Division Officer was defending him, and the skipper learned that the Division Officer too was somewhat accountable. Needham almost placed him in hack. The 3M (PMS) Coordinator was almost hyperventilating. I mean the crap was hitting the fan everywhere. I only wish I had taped it. To make a long story shorter, they were both found guilty and busted. But to humiliate them on the ships TV? What a jerk!

That's what I meant about the Indy's morale. Even in 1988 when we were in Gitmo, the Fleet Training Center told Needham that there was no morale on the ship. It was awful.

I discharged on Jan.11, 1991 as a second class petty officer. My work center supervisor told me he didn't blame me for getting out because of the morale. But he assured me, it wasn't like on other ships like it was on the INDY. I'm sure he was right, but I had no incentive to find out for sure.

Donald:

Brian, that ship did have some bad morale when I came on board. It never got any better. Those people that worked for me were all depressed. It was like someone had threatened them with all kinds of stupid punishments and then didn't follow through and then threatened them again. I tried to pull them all up, but it seems like every time I got things going in a positive flow someone in my department would do something stupid where I had to send them to Captain's Mast. That then brought them and all their friends down on me.

I am the type who feels that everyone should be held accountable for their actions. I have always held myself accountable, so why not everyone else. If you aren't going to hold yourself accountable for your actions, then I will if you work for me.

That is the reason I didn't mind jumping on senior officers about their actions. Sometimes I would be verbally reprimanded by being told that I was not a loyal officer. I would always come back with, "Dogs are loyal even if you beat them. Men become loyal if the leader earns their respect." I will not give a boss of mine respect until he shows me that he will stick up for me when I am in the right, reprimand me when I am wrong and is totally honest at all times.

I have never had a problem getting my people to do things for me because I am a servant first and a leader second.

It is too bad that you had the problems that you had. You sound like a great guy with good morals and ethics. I would have been privileged to have you work for me.

More Gundecking

Brian:

Another incident was in 1989. I was a newly frocked third class petty officer. There was this second class that treated all airmen (E-1 to E-3) like total dirt. He wouldn't trust them to do maintenance on anything without the supervision of at least a third class petty officer or above.

His name was Fred Mitchell. We called him "laser breath" because his breath stunk. I mean it was awful.

He had been in the Navy a good 12 years. We were in V-2 waist catapults. He was the Cat 3 captain. They were doing maintenance on Cat 3 and after a check was done, the chief discovered that ABE2 Mitchell gundecked 9 PMS checks.

He was charged immediately, court-martialed, sent to the brig and then discharged. What a hypocrite. He wouldn't trust an airman because of his rank. To me that was some type of bigotry.

Boot campers are just new people. Some had aspirations of making the Navy a career. If you treat them like dirt on account of their short time in service, you can't blame them for counting the days.

Speaking of maintenance, do you remember when the Indy was a week late pulling out of San Diego for our West Pac deployment which led us to "Operation Desert Shield"? That was Cat 4.

I was in V-2 maintenance support. That was about a 200 man operation. That assignment is what got me the Navy Achievement Medal from Captain Ellis.

To this day, I know that there were personnel from my division who deserved it more than me. I felt guilty taking it. We had to keep that assignment quiet all week. Shipmates from every department would ask us when Cat 4 will be done so we can deploy for Hawaii. Bos'n Tracey ordered us all to keep it in the division.

Remember Desert Shield? 111 consecutive days at sea. Did you ever top that ever, man? That was discipline. I still tell that to people today. I don't know too many Navy vets who can tell me they spent more consecutive days at sea than that not to mention the heat. That heat in the gulf was the worst.

Donald:

As for the Desert Shield cruise, do I remember it? You bet I do. That was a cruise that I will always remember. I didn't stay put onboard in the Gulf. My little ensign and I took turns flying on and off to pick up classified stuff and then delivering classified stuff to ships in the Gulf and to other places like Bahrain, Muscat, Oman, then flew to the USNS Mercy (I think that was the hospital ship out there.) twice. I also remember after leaving Bahrain one time in a helo that we had to make a stop at Prince Sultan Air Base to pick up a plane part. They did not have the plane part ready for pick up. We ended up sitting on that hot tarmac for over 2 hours waiting for the part. They would not let us out of the helo for security reasons. By the time we got back to the ship from that trip I was dehydrated.

Dumb Pilots

Donald:

I also remember some dumb pilots who caused problems in Hawaii on the way over who tore up a hotel room and Captain Bixler, the XO, wanted all wardroom officers to help pay for the $7,000 damage. I spoke up and told them that since I did not participate in the parties in that room that I was not going to pay for damages that I did not cause. All of a sudden other officers spoke up and said the same thing. The officers who caused the problem ended up paying for the damages out of their own pockets. They made some sort of deal with the hotel to pay the damages off in payments.

Then on the way back from the Gulf on our stopover in Singapore, several of the squadrons and the ships company wardroom rented some suites at the Singapore Hilton and partied down. I went into one of the suites to see what was going on and guess what was going on? A few of the pilots were drunk and were trying to see if they could hit the swimming pool from 28 stories up with a full beer can. I told those idiots that if they missed the swimming pool as someone was walking by, they could kill them. Someone did call security and as I was walking out of the room, security was on its way to the room. I helped them get their quicker by pointing out the room.

Brian:

That was stupid when you consider how strict their (Singapore) judicial system is. Bos'n Tracey warned us the day before we pulled in that we couldn't go wild like we did in the Philippines. Those pilots could have been in huge trouble. That at sea period (Desert Shield) may have warranted some craziness. I simply stayed by myself and ate in quiet restaurants in their malls. It was nice just to be in civilization again.

During my ordeal (with the Marines) I was so appreciative of CDR McEwen, the XO. He was the only officer who was really interested in learning the truth much more than the Master Chief or Needham. McEwen was fair and open-minded and so was LCDR Rolph.

It was such a shame that some of the leaders thought that they had to be pricks to lead people.

On a carrier, you find all kinds as I'm sure you know. I remember two petty officers from Hawaii. One became my catapult captain. Unlike some petty officers who would say "You're working for him; or you're working for me." My cat captain always told us that "you're not working for me; you're working with me, and I'll be working with you." His name was ABE2 Kanaeholo. His nickname was "Ape". That's the approach petty officers needed to take. He went on to be a company commander at Recruit Training Command in San Diego.

The other one, ABE2 Helsham, worked in arresting gear. He never minded getting his hands dirty and doing the hard work, but he demanded that everyone under his watch to match his energy. No more, no less. I always respected those guys. We became good friends.

Farewell to Needham

Brian:

Trust me, you would have hated Needham.

True story, (like all of mine). On Feb 2nd, 1989, the INDY was celebrating her 30th birthday. All crewmembers (except of course the duty section) were invited to a formal banquet in San Diego.

I forgot the name of the restaurant or hotel, but officers and chiefs wore their dress blues and the dress for enlisted was optional. We were all having a grand time.

Then the admiral of COMNAVAIRPAC made a formal announcement that Captain "Buzz" Needham was leaving the Indy by the end of February. The entire ballroom cheered like it was a game winning home run in a World Series or a touchdown in the Super Bowl.

Needham was standing next to the admiral observing this celebration of his departure. I mean right in front of him. All I could do was laugh. I hadn't gotten over the way he let Corporal Rosinsky walk away from an assault with a deadly weapon charge. I mean he was hated everywhere, so much for an Annapolis grad. I almost felt sorry for him. I have a picture of myself with Buzz Needham the day I got frocked to petty officer third class. It was 2 months since that mast on the foc'sle. I didn't smile with him, especially when that jerk Master Chief Stone announced my name. He gave me a second look before he did so and said "oh oh" before he said my name.

I can't tell you how much I hated him more at that time.

Donald:

Brian, do not ever change. You have good morals and ethics. That is a quality that is missing among American men these days. Never lie, never cover up. It will eventually come back to get you.

I had a chapter in my first book entitled "Morals and Ethics" and I talk about some of those incidents.

I felt I was wronged a couple of times and when I received a bad fitness report (officer performance evaluation), I tried to get it either erased from my record or the reporting officer to amend it. I could never get that done, because the Board for Corrections of Naval Records told me that my letter was written in a way to impugn the motives of others. So I had to work extra hard just to get promoted to LT. I was passed over once for LT, because of those bad reports.

Note: This story is made up of excerpts from e-mails passed back and forth over a period of about two weeks. All events and names are as we remember them and are only opinions of each of us. We both feel that bad leadership will lead to morale problems and that is something that our military does not need. The Armed Forces sometimes do not weed out the bad leaders before they get into positions of authority that affect the lives of the men and women below them. I feel the Armed Forces need to revise their leadership training so that they can identify those enlisted and commissioned officers who are bad leaders and keep them from holding positions that could adversely affect the livelihood of those below them. The Armed Forces needs leaders that will listen, that are honest and that will stand up for you when you are in the right. They need to be Fair, Balanced and Honest. Donald Johnson

Chapter 9

Special Tributes to the American Sailor

In this chapter I have included tributes to our military and I also have a speech that I gave in my early days of speech making about an Admiral that I once met when he was the Chief of Naval Personnel, a man who helped me out of a bad situation.

> *"At this place, at this Memorial, we acknowledge a debt of long-standing to an entire generation of Americans: those who died; those who fought and worked and grieved and went on. They saved our country, and thereby saved the liberty of mankind. And now I ask every man and woman who saw and lived World War II—every member of that generation—to please rise as you are able, and receive the thanks of our great nation."*
>   —President George W.
>   Bush at the dedication of the World War II Memorial

> *On Memorial Day, America undertakes its solemn duty to remember the sacred list of brave Americans who have sacrificed their lives for the cause of freedom and the security of our nation. By honoring these proud soldiers, sailors, airmen, Marines, and Coast Guardsmen lost throughout our country's history, we renew our commitment to upholding the democratic ideals they fought and died to preserve.*
>   —President Bush on Memorial Day 2003

Ode to a Long Lost Shipmate
By Author Unknown
Contributed by Donald Johnson

'Twas a day so many long years ago,
When I first met some men, whom I grew to know.
It was then at a time when we were at war.
And off went these men to a foreign shore!
For almost two years they share their life.
With man's two worst evils, war and strife.
They lived their lives as close to another,
And became to each one just like a brother.
They fought the long war with all that they had,
Through invasions, bombings and air raids as bad.
Some of these men, death did certainly spurn,
And many to life they did not return.
And then the war was a thing of the past,
They went home to their loved ones, a life to be cast.
Forging through years with their hopes to survive,
And to make the new Democracy thrive.
Many years later in our empty old nest,
A thought came to mind: What became of the rest?
Of those whom we spent every war-time fear,
And to find them, and to share our memories so clear.
After looking through books for many an hour.
Service records and letters we did certainly scour.
And then we found some names long gone by,
We let out a yell, and then we did cry.
So many a month of searching was past.
We had found some shipmates at very long last
For now our lives are finally joined once more.
Together with hope as we returned to this shore.
From men who had left with much unending fears,
Are now enjoying their final few years.
Still hope that they have passed along,
Some help to the world they had fought for so long.
That some gave their lives to help us be great,
While others that are left, can only await,
The Time when our GOD does say at the end,
"WELL DONE, THOU TRUE AND FAITHFUL FRIEND!"

A MAN OF INTEGRITY
By Donald Johnson
Copyright © 1996

*This is a speech that I gave at my Toastmasters club in May 1996 not to long after
Admiral Boorda committed suicide.*

Does the media go too far? It did this time! It went too far especially when it
came to one man that I have so dearly admired for over 14 years. That man was
Admiral Mike Boorda. He was a man of integrity, a man loved by many a sailor
and officer. He was a man who joined the Navy after a hard childhood, who
worked his way from the enlisted ranks to officer status, better known as a
mustang officer, to become the top executive of the U.S. Navy, a feat never done
by any enlisted man before him. He was a man who cared for his sailors and
officers and their families. He did much to bring about a better Navy for everyone when he was the Chief of Naval Personnel and continued to make progress
in that area when he became the Chief of Naval Operations. He once saved me
from a verbally abusive commanding officer and executive officer while I was
stationed on Adak Island in the Aleutians. I talked to him personally on the
telephone. He promised to find me a good seagoing command to get my career
back into shape. He did that. He saved my Navy officer career. I also found out
just recently that he played a major role in re-assigning that commanding officer and executive officer and by forcing them into early retirement. I owed him
not once but twice for those actions.

How many of you believe most of what the media puts out on TV, radio and
the newswires and magazines? How many of you would believe the media if
they did an expose on a friend of yours, on something that maybe you didn't
know anything about that person? How many of you?

Well, Mr. Toastmaster, fellow Toastmasters and guests, a survey taken by the
Hoover Institute a few years ago indicated that 85% of the population believes
everything put out by the media, a media that is very slanted to the far left. A
media that wants to control what we do in everyday life. How well that can
happen if they are in control of the population.

I have been an outspoken critic of the media for years. Even before I retired
from the Navy as a mustang Lieutenant, I was critical of the major news

anchors, Dan Rather, Peter Jennings and Tom Brokaw. I had a lot of respect for John Chancellor until he criticized General Norman Schwarzkopf on how he was conducting the Persian Gulf War. I got to meet Dan Rather in the Gulf along with Generals Schwarzkopf and Powell. Dan Rather was out to make a name for himself and to bring his ratings back up to where they once were. Peter Arnett of CNN who spent the entire Gulf War in a hotel in Baghdad was out to make a name for himself and to increase the ratings for his network. He did just that. To me he is a traitor to America. He reported on things that I thought were anti-military/anti-Persian Gulf war. He showed the horrors of war and made it look like we were the bad guys.

Why do reporters and editors try to break the spirit of good people? Two such people did just that in the case of Mike Boorda. The reporter was a disgruntled retired Marine. Did he have some sort of grudge to pick with the military and wanted to try to ruin the career of the beloved CNO or was he just out to make a name for himself. Who cares about a couple of Bronze V's? That reporter had to dig deep and for a long time in order to get that kind of dirt. The Admiral was questioned over a year ago about his Vietnam earned medals and the Bronze Combat V on a couple of them. He quit wearing them after that because he was not sure if he did earn them. He wanted to keep the integrity that he had built with his sailors and officers. Why did this reporter still want to interview the Admiral even after he quit wearing the Bronze V's? Nobody else really cared. I believe this reporter was out to ruin this man, a man of integrity. Integrity is something this reporter probably knows little about.

Admiral Mike Boorda did see action in Vietnam. As the weapons officer aboard destroyer USS John Craig in 1965, he directed gunfire at enemy targets ashore in Vietnam. He was providing combat support to the troops ashore. Even if he was sitting off shore, his ship was still susceptible to enemy fire from ashore. It took a lot of courage for anyone to be in any situation over there, whether it was in the rice paddies or sitting on a destroyer off the coast. When he was awarded certain medals for his duties in Vietnam, maybe a mistake was made in the service record entry indicating that he could wear a Bronze V for valor in combat. But in my eyes and probably in the eyes of all promotion board members after that he deserved it.

There was one other media situation that same week that might have pushed Admiral Boorda to suicide just before that interview with that disrespectful reporter.

A bitter naval officer, recently relieved of command because of crew abuse, hid behind anonymity to launch a personal attack at the Admiral. In a letter published in the Navy Times signed "Name Withheld", this officer claimed no one respected Admiral Boorda any longer, that behind his back fellow admirals called him "Little Mikey Boorda." This was a lie, of course. I think he knew it. But would his sailors?

Now why did the editor of the Navy Times print that letter signed "Name Withheld". I do not think any letter should be published anywhere in any publication unless the author is willing to have their name attached to that letter or article especially if it is an article that is trying to defame someone. It is not fair to the person being defamed.

I think what happened to this man of integrity is that his high spirit was finally broken. He took over a Navy full of scandal after the Tailhook convention in Las Vegas. He also had to deal with other sexual harassment incidents and the loss of several million dollar fighter jets and the deployment of ships to trouble spots around the world. Maybe all of these highly publicized incidents and events began to tame his spirit. He cared for his sailors and officers and their families very, very much. These two media events coming at about the same time probably broke his spirit. Anytime you break the spirit of a human being, you have lost that person to the human race, whether to suicide or to a mental ward somewhere. These media events were going to be questioning his integrity and that would bring on another scandal in the Navy and with his position. With his spirit being broken, he probably did not want another major scandal. I think that he was not going to give the media a chance to do that. The Navy has endured too many scandals in the past 10 years and he has tried his best to bring the integrity of the Navy back to where it was in World War II. Committing suicide was his way to save face for himself as well as for his Navy. Admiral Mike Boorda is now a martyr. I will do what I have to do to change the media. I will try my best to get that disrespectful reporter banned from reporting or having anything published in the media ever again and I am going to petition the Navy Times to not publish anonymous letters. I feel if you aren't man or woman enough to sign your name to a published article or book then your article or book isn't worth publishing.

I am talking about taking away free speech from those two. As far as I am concerned, they were infringing on the rights of the Admiral his right to be free from assault, verbal assault. I feel when you violate the rights of others that your rights should be taken away for the rest of your life. Admiral Boorda no longer has any rights. He is dead.

I want each and every one of you sitting here today to look at the media in a more critical way and do not believe everything you read or see or hear. The media only publishes what they want you to read, see or hear.

Dale Carnegie said that "Any fool can criticize, condemn and complain—and most fools do." These two people were fools.

Consider this: Be respectful of the other person, and always keep him or her in mind. Treat other people with the same respect with which you want to be treated.

My last comment is to Admiral Mike Boorda:

Admiral, do not worry about what happens to Seaman Jones and his wife and his kids. They will be taken care of by those sailors and officers that you helped in the past. The Navy will survive partly because of the leadership you provided and the caring attitude that you showed to your sailors and officers. I am with you now in spirit and I will pray for your family and your Navy. Godspeed in your heavenly endeavors. Your name will live on.

I Was a Sailor Once
By Author Unknown
Contributed by Donald Johnson

Sharing a glimpse of the life I so dearly loved…

I liked standing on the bridge wing at sunrise with salt spray in my face and clean ocean winds whipping in from the four quarters of the globe—

I liked the sounds of the Navy—the piercing trill of the boatswains pipe, the syncopated clangor of the ship's bell on the quarterdeck, harsh, and the strong language and laughter of sailors at work.

I liked Navy vessels—plodding fleet auxiliaries,—ATF 76 USS Ute—and amphibs, sleek submarines and steady solid aircraft carriers.

I liked the proud names of Navy ships: Midway, Lexington, Saratoga, Coral Sea, Antietam, Valley Forge—memorials of great battles won and tribulations overcome.

I liked the lean angular names of Navy "tin-cans" and escorts—DD 731 USS Maddox—mementos of heroes who went before us.

And the others—San Jose, San Diego, Los Angeles, St. Paul, Chicago, Oklahoma City, named for our cities.

I liked the tempo of a Navy band .

I liked liberty call and the spicy scent of a foreign port.

I even liked the never ending paperwork and all hands working parties as my ship filled herself with the multitude of supplies, both mundane and to cut ties to the land and carry out her mission anywhere on the globe where there was water to float her.

I liked sailors, officers and enlisted men from all parts of the land, farms of the Midwest, small towns of New England, from the cities, the mountains and the prairies, from all walks of life. I trusted and depended on them as they trusted and depended on me—for professional competence, for comradeship, for strength and courage. In a word, they were "shipmates"; then and forever.

I liked the surge of adventure in my heart, when the word was passed: "Now Hear This" "Now set the special sea and anchor detail—all hands to quarters for leaving port," and I liked the infectious thrill of sighting home again, with the waving hands of welcome from family and friends waiting pier side

The work was hard and dangerous; the going rough at times; the parting from loved ones painful, but the companionship of robust Navy laughter, the "all for one and one for all" philosophy of the sea was ever present.

I liked the serenity of the sea after a day of hard ship's work, as flying fish flitted across the wave tops and sunset gave way to night.

I liked the feel of the Navy in darkness—the masthead and range lights, the red and green navigation lights and stern light, the pulsating phosphorescence of radar repeaters—they cut through the dusk and joined with the mirror of stars overhead. And I liked drifting off to sleep lulled by the myriad noises large and small that told me that my ship was alive and well, and that my shipmates on watch would keep me safe.

I liked quiet mid-watches with the aroma of strong coffee—the lifeblood of the Navy permeating everywhere.

And I liked hectic watches when the exacting minuet of haze-gray shapes racing at flank speed kept all hands on a razor edge of alertness.

I liked the sudden electricity of "General quarters, general quarters, all hands man your battle stations," followed by the hurried clamor of running feet on ladders and the resounding thump of watertight doors as the ship transformed herself in a few brief seconds from a peaceful workplace to a weapon of war—ready for anything.

And I liked the sight of space-age equipment manned by youngsters clad in dungarees and sound-powered phones that their grandfathers would still recognize

I liked the traditions of the Navy and the men and women who made them. I liked the proud names of Navy heroes: Halsey, Nimitz, Perry, Farragut, John

Paul Jones and Burke. A sailor could find much in the Navy: comrades-in-arms, pride in self and country, mastery of the seaman's trade. An adolescent could find adulthood.

In years to come, when sailors are home from the sea, AND SO WE ARE,—We still remember with fondness and respect the ocean in all its moods—the impossible shimmering mirror calm and the storm-tossed green water surging over the bow. And then there will come again a faint whiff of stack gas, a faint echo of engine and rudder orders, a vision of the bright bunting of signal flags snapping at the yardarm, a refrain of hearty laughter in the wardroom and chief's quarters and mess decks.

Gone ashore for good we grow humble about our Navy days, when the seas were a part of us and a new port of call was ever over the horizon.

Remembering this, WE stand taller and say, " I WAS A SAILOR ONCE."

What is a Mustang?
by Donald Johnson

In the Navy, a Mustang is an Officer who has promoted up from the ranks of Navy enlisted personnel through an in-service procurement program, with no interruption of his/her active duty status. It is also understood that the Mustang Officer was a career Sailor, and normally wears one or more Good Conduct Medals.

Thus, the Navy Mustang is either a Navy Limited Duty Officers (LDO), a Chief Warrant Officers (CWO), or commissioned through the Direct Fleet Accession, Seaman to Admiral (S2A) program, or through the Enlisted Commissioning Program. In the past, there were other programs leading to a commission, such as NESEP, or the Naval Flight Officer program, but these have since gone away.

LDO's and CWO's are a very unique part of the Naval service. The LDO or CWO serves in a role like no other commissioned officer can. LDOs and CWOs are enlisted people who are commissioned as Officers, and have been called to serve from their senior enlisted ranks as technical managers. An LDO or CWO has the necessary experience and technical background to perform tasks that call for the "officer" rank and protocol to carry out, but require the enlisted heart and experience to get accomplished. Currently, the US Navy and Marine Corps are the only branches of the armed forces to have such commissioning programs in place.

The term "Mustang" is a relatively modern term, originating either just prior to, or during World War II. It is believed to be a Sea Service term, although other service officers are beginning to be described as Mustangs.

It literally refers to the mustang horse, which is a wild animal and therefore not a thoroughbred. A mustang, after being captured, can be tamed and saddle broken but it always has a bit of wild streak, and can periodically revert to its old ways unexpectedly and therefore the owner needs to keep an eye on it at all times.

By the same token, however, since a mustang was formerly a wild and free animal, it may very well be smarter, more capable and have a better survival instinct than thoroughbreds. The mustang can take care of itself when things get tough, thriving on rough treatment, while the thoroughbred, having been pampered its whole life, cannot.

You can easily see the parallel between horses and Naval Officers. The term "Mustang" is used in a complimentary sense most of the time.

An LDO or CWO is an officer by appearance and in the minds of the "top brass," and an enlisted technician at heart. The creed of the LDO/CWO, upon receiving their commission is: "I did it the hard way...I earned it."

Chapter 10

Patriotic Stories

People have written patriotic stories, speeches and poems since the earliest of wars. The 20th and 21st centuries are no different. In this chapter, you will find stories, speeches and poems.

> *"Moral cowardice that keeps us from speaking our minds is as dangerous to this country as irresponsible talk. The right way is not always the popular and easy way. Standing for right when it is unpopular is a true test of moral character."*
> —Margaret Chase Smith

> *Don't be a fool and die for your country. Let the other sonofabitch die for his.*
> —General George Patton

> *I do not mean to exclude altogether the idea of patriotism. I know it exists, and I know it has done much in the present contest. But I will venture to assert, that a great and lasting war can never be supported on this principle alone. It must be aided by a prospect of interest, or some reward.*
> —George Washington

Our American Symbol
By Donald Johnson
Copyright © 1992

This is one of the first speeches that I had ever given as a Toastmaster. I have come a long way since then.

"I pledge allegiance to the flag of the United States of America and to the republic for which it stands, one nation **under God**, indivisible with liberty and justice for all."

Mr. Toastmaster, Fellow Toastmasters and most honored guests.

Our American Symbol, the flag of the United States of America.

How many of you take pride in reciting the pledge to our flag?

I feel many people just go through the motions and don't have any feelings.

Not me! I take pride each and every time I say the pledge.

I can remember when I first started Kindergarten; the first thing we did was all stand, place our hand over our heart and recite the pledge. I was so proud on that day nearly 50 years ago.

I began to see some degradation in the American people's pride of the flag during the Vietnam War. I felt that the flag burnings on college campuses were wrong. I do not think that those students knew what they were doing. Were they protesting against our American symbol or were they protesting against foreign policy? You all know the answer, now! There are ways to protest American foreign policy other than burning a symbol that had nothing to do with our presence there. Don't burn the flag! Burn the politicians in effigy. They are the ones who put the military into combat. Write them. Become pro-active in politics. There is a movement to amend the constitution making it unlawful to desecrate the American Flag. I personally do not want to see another amendment, but if it is going to keep people from burning our symbol of freedom I am all for it. I want to see a revival of pride in our American flag.

I am going to take you back to three historical eras where I feel the flag helped to instill some pride and brought hope to many people of the world.

The first era was not too long ago. The flag you see in my Navy retirement shadow box was flown above the USS Independence, an aircraft carrier, during the Persian Gulf conflict. That flag to me and many other American people is a symbol of freedom, a symbol of freedom not only to us Americans but a symbol of freedom to many other people of the world including the people of Kuwait. The Persian Gulf coalition led by the United States of America regained their freedom. I am very proud to own a flag that was flown during that conflict.

The American flag has also helped our POWs endure unjust torture. The second era was Vietnam. Retired Vice Admiral Stockdale, who was the senior Navy POW in North Vietnam, received the Medal of Honor for his courage and leadership. One thing that kept his hopes alive was a daily vision of the American flag, the thirteen stripes and 50 white stars on a blue background. He knew that America would be waiting on him when he was released. My hat is off to Vice Admiral Stockdale for maintaining his pride in the American Flag and for keeping his faith in America.

How many of you are keeping track of the 50 year anniversaries of WWII battles? My Uncle Don Johnson was a Navy boat coxswain and dropped Marines off at the beaches of Iwo Jima the same place that Joe Rosenthal of San Francisco took that Pulitzer Prize winning photo of 5 Marines and 1 Navy Corpsman raising the American flag on top of Mt. Suribachi. That battle cost the Marines more casualties than any other battle in history. That photo was used in preparing the sculpture for the Marine Corps Memorial in Washington, DC. That stirring image of the raising of the flag on Iwo Jima has become one of the cornerstones for our country's patriotism and pride in our American symbol.

I want each and every one of you to think back to when you first learned the Pledge of Allegiance. If you are a new American, learn the Pledge and be proud of it and what it stands for. The American flag has helped many veterans survive battles and stints in POW camps knowing that America will still be there when they get back. I want each and every one of my fellow Americans to feel pride each and every time that they say the Pledge of Allegiance. I will end by quoting Capt. William Driver. Upon seeing, the American Flag raised over his ship off Salem, Massachusetts, in December, 1831 he said, "There it is—Old Glory!"

I Am Coming!
By Author Unknown
Contributed by Vern Bluhm

Dear Terrorists,

I am a Navy Aviator. I was born and raised in a small town in New England. I come from a family of five. I was raised in a middle class home and was taught my values by my mother and father.

My dad worked a series of jobs in finance and my mom took care of us kids. We were not an overly religious family but attended church most Sundays. It was a nice small Episcopal Church. I have a brother and sister and I am the youngest in my family. I was the first in many generations to attend college.

I have flown Naval aircraft for 16 years. For me the flying was never a lifelong dream or a "calling," it just happened. I needed a job and I liked the challenge. I continue to do it today because I feel it is important to give back to a nation, which has given so much to me. I do it because, although I will never be rich, my family will be comfortable.

I do it because many of my friends have left for the airlines and someone has to do it.

My government has spent millions to train me to fly these multi-million dollar aircrafts. I make about 70,000 dollars a year and after 20 years will be offered a pension.

I like baseball but think the players make too much money. I am in awe of firemen and policemen and what they do each day for my community, and like teachers, they just do not get paid enough.

I respect my elders and always use sir or ma'am when addressing a stranger. I am not sure about kids these days but I think that is normal for every generation.

I tell you all this because when I come for you, I want you to know me. I will not be hiding behind a woman or a child. I will not be disguised or pretending to be something, I am not. I will be in a U.S. issue flight suit. I will be wearing standard US issue flight gear, and I will be flying a navy aircraft clearly marked as a US warplane. I wish we could meet up close in a small room where I could wrap my hands around your throat and slowly squeeze the life out of you, but unfortunately, you're hiding in a hole in the ground, so we will have to do this a different way.

I want you to know also that I am very good at what I do. I can put a 2,000 lb weapon through a window from 10,000 feet up. I generally only fly at night, so you may want to start sleeping during the day. I am not eager to die for my country but I am willing to sacrifice my life to protect it from animals like you.

I will do everything in my power to ensure no civilians are hurt as I take aim at you.

My countrymen are a forgiving bunch. Many are already forgetting what you did on Sept 11th. But I will not forget!!

I am coming! I hope you know me a little bit better, see you soon…sleep tight.

Signed

A U.S. Navy Pilot

Our Soldiers, Sailors, Airmen and Marines are a few of our greatest assets!
God Bless

THE DEFENSE OF FREEDOM
By Donald Johnson
Copyright © 1996

This speech was given at one of many Toastmasters meetings in 1996.

Don Johnson!! Not me! Not Sonny Crockett or Nash Bridges! But my grandfather, the first of three Don Johnsons in my family.

My Grandfather was a Swede, first generation born in America, in the small farming community of Randolph, Kansas. He played football in high school and showed me his wounds suffered in a league championship game played in 1917. He was going to follow in his fathers footsteps and become a farmer. World War I changed that forever. He enlisted in the Army and was sent to France as part of the American Expeditionary Forces in an Army Resupply Division. He worked with the Marines at the Battle of Belleau Wood and was awarded three combat medals which included the Purple Heart. He was later wounded in a mustard gas attack when his gas mask failed to operate properly. He was sent home with seared lungs. This injury plagued him for the rest of his life.

My grandfather went to war, the war to end all wars. He went to war in the defense of freedom.

His oldest son, Seth, was in the Army in the Philippines and was taken captive and served the rest of the war as a prisoner of war (POW). His second son, the second of three Don Johnsons, was a coxswain mate during World War II. During WWII, he served on ships during the Battles of Iwo Jima and Okinawa. The third son, my father, served in the Army at Camp Gordon, GA during the Korean War. The fourth son, Gene, was a Marine serving in Korea fighting in three of the many battles of Pork Chop Hill and received 2 Purple Hearts for his battles. His fifth son, Cordon was a boatswain mate and ship's serviceman (barber) in the Navy during the early 50s to early 60s. While his sixth son, Dwane served as a specialist in the Army in the late 50s. His daughter married a career sailor who served in Korea and Vietnam. All of his sons and son-in-law served in the defense of freedom.

My mother's three brothers also served in the armed forces. Her oldest brother, Herb, served in the Navy on an escort aircraft carrier and in support of the troops fighting in Okinawa. Her middle brother, Dean, served in the Army during the Korean War while her youngest brother was a Cold War warrior with the Marine Corps. All served in the defense of freedom.

I served both in Vietnam and in the Persian Gulf conflict in the defense of freedom. I served on board five different ships during my 20 years. One of those was an amphibious assault ship that carried helicopters, landing craft and 3,000 Marines. That ship was named after the battle that my grandfather fought in. It was the USS Belleau Wood. It is still in commission today, forward deployed to its homeport of Sasebo, Japan. My last duty station was on board USS Independence, an aircraft carrier now forward deployed to its home port of Yokosuka, JA. Guess what it was named for.

My sister joined the Naval Reserves and went to war. She served in Saudi Arabia about 20 miles from the front lines of Kuwait. She was part of a combat cargo handling battalion. She offloaded and onloaded the roll-on/roll-off ships for the Marines and Army. Her husband was an active duty sailor for about nine years and later became a reservist as a SeaBee operating heavy equipment. Both of them served in the defense of freedom.

On Monday I went to a Toastmasters meeting in Dixon. The theme of the meeting was keyed towards Veteran's Day. I sat and listened to 12 people stand up and speak from 2-22 minutes on some subject dealing with Veteran's Day. Some told stories about their military career. Some told about their family's military heritage. And others talked about someone they knew who served. One lady spoke about how her heart went out to all the veterans who had served and returned home to live, while others gave their lives. She had a hard time coping with the art of war. She said she had all the respect in the world for our veterans but if her brother was ever drafted and was going to be sent off to war, she would do everything in her power to keep him from going because she did not want to deal with the thought that he may not come home alive.

That really got me to thinking especially after I had spoken about my hero, my Grandpa Johnson. My thoughts rolled back to an article that I had recently read in an American Legion magazine titled "The Defense of Freedom". It talked about all of the wars we had been in since the First World War and how warfare and weapons technology advanced. It also talked about how women and blacks helped in the Second World War. John Stevens, a professor of history at the Indiana University School of Liberal Arts stated, "The war was won using a segregated army to save democracy—a sad irony."

The article went on to say, "Many wonder why the United States wars so often, and so far from home. Foreign tyrants rarely pose a direct threat to America, true, but they do pose a threat to American principles. The United States always has served as the model for liberty. Perhaps that is why America feels so bound by honor to pick up the gauntlet on behalf of the free world. Perhaps, because of the diversity that comes from a nation peopled with descendants of Europeans, Africans and Asians, Americans rush to their aid from an innate sense of loyalty." I think that we should leave the reasons to the philosophers.

The thing that really struck me about listening to those speakers were the number of people who had served, the number of relatives who had served and came home alive and the number of relatives who gave their lives in the name of freedom.

This article indicated that 116,000 Americans died overseas during the United States' 18 months of involvement in World War I. 406,000 Americans sacrificed their lives in World War II. The first warming of the Cold War began on the Korean peninsula June 25, 1950. Officially, the "United Nations police action" ended five years later with more than 50,000 confirmed American deaths and another 8,176 missing. Just a decade after the Korean War, the United States took action elsewhere in Asia: Vietnam. In what became the longest official war involving the United States, battle lines gave way to body counts. "Here U.S. military leaders had to relearn guerrilla warfare, having forgotten the Indian Wars and the Philippine insurrection." A dramatically different approach to combat, but the results were no less painful. Instead of reports on how much land was secured, young lieutenants provided casualty counts as proof of victory—victories that cost 58,000 Americans.

Limited actions occurred in Lebanon, Grenada and Panama to achieve limited aims. Cost: 305 dead, 514 wounded. Once again, war on grand scale erupted on Aug 2, 1990 when Saddam Hussein's Iraqi forces invaded the tiny nation of Kuwait. More than 383 U.S. soldiers lost their lives to uphold borders in that region. In Somalia, U.S. forces attempted to feed the hungry, with 44 Americans slain for their intrusion into domestic affairs of the Somali people. We have yet to complete the count of Americans who have given their lives in Bosnia.

I knew many lives had been given in all of those military actions, but it never really hit me like it did the other night. I have had all types of feelings over the years, but none like I felt the other night when I heard this young lady speak. I had a feeling of empathy and sympathy for all of those families who had lost someone in war. I had to cry right along with her. I think we all cried that night. I will now forever look at Veteran's Day in a different light. I will have more respect for our fellow veterans, alive and dead, than ever. I lost two close friends in Vietnam and I do not think that I ever grieved for them until the other night. Now I can go on with life and know that my two friends did not die in vain.

I came from a family rich in military tradition. I was the first career military man. If duty ever calls again and I am recalled to active duty to serve, I will do so. I despise war, but I will fight to defend the freedoms of our country.

Thomas Jefferson said, "My views and feelings (are) in favor of the abolition of war—and I hope it is practicable, by improving the mind and morals of society, to lessen the disposition to war; but of its abolition I despair."

John Stevens states, "Spoken nearly two centuries ago, these words continue to ring true. Nonetheless, while few long for war, history shows a propensity for conflict. When it has come, U.S. citizens from every walk of life have answered the call to arms and come to defend American ideals around the globe. They will continue to do so—in defense of freedom."

A Deck of Cards
By Author Unknown
Contributed by Donald Johnson

It was quiet that day, the guns and the mortars, and land mines for some reason had not been heard. The young soldier knew it was Sunday, the holiest day of the week.

As he was sitting there, he got out an old deck of cards and laid them out across his bunk.

Just then, an army sergeant came in and said, "Why aren't you with the rest of the platoon?

The soldier replied, "I thought I would stay behind and spend some time with the Lord."

The sergeant said, "Looks to me like you're going to play cards."

The soldier said, "No, sir. You see, since we are not allowed to have Bibles or other spiritual books in this country, I've decided to talk to the Lord by studying this deck of cards."

The sergeant asked in disbelief, "How will you do that?"

You see the Ace, Sergeant? It reminds me that there is only one God.

The Two represents the two parts of the Bible, Old and New Testaments.

The Three represents the Father, Son, and the Holy Ghost.

The Four stands for the Four Gospels: Matthew, Mark, Luke and John.

The Five is for the five virgins that were ten but only five of them were glorified.

The Six is for the six days it took God to create the Heavens and Earth.

The Seven is for the day God rested after making His Creation.

The Eight is for the family of Noah and his wife, their three sons and their wives—the eight people God spared from the flood that destroyed the earth.

The Nine is for the lepers that Jesus cleansed of leprosy. He cleansed ten, but nine never thanked Him.

The Ten represents the Ten Commandments that God handed down to Moses on tablets made of stone.

The Jack is a reminder of Satan, one of God's first angels, but he got kicked out of heaven for his sly and wicked ways and is now the joker of eternal hell.

The Queen stands for the Virgin Mary.

The King stands for Jesus, for he is the King of all kings.

When I count the dots on all the cards, I come up with 365 total, one for every day of the year.

There are a total of 52 cards in a deck; each is a week—52 weeks in a year.

The four suits represent the four seasons: Spring, Summer, Fall and Winter.

Each suit has thirteen cards there are exactly thirteen weeks in a quarter

So when I want to talk to God and thank Him, I just pull out this old deck of cards and they remind me of all that I have to be thankful for"

The sergeant just stood there. After a minute, with tears in his eyes and pain in his heart, he said, "Soldier, may I borrow that deck of cards?"

Please let this be a reminder and take time to pray for all of our soldiers, sailors, airmen and marines who are being sent away, putting their lives on the line fighting for us!

When a Soldier Dies
By Jim Willis
©2005 Jim Willis

When a Soldier dies many miles from home
Leaving friends and family to wonder alone
Who will go to where they lie
to say good words when a Soldier dies?

When a Soldier dies we ponder then
What might they have done, what might they have been?
But in our grief, our shock and our cries,
We are simply numb when a Soldier dies

When a Soldier dies we measure the pain
Did they fight for freedom? Did they die in vain?
The answers are important you can't deny
to these questions we ask when a Soldier dies

When a Soldier dies we think of a way
To remember forever the year and the day
That they gave their life and we think with a sigh
We'll never forget when a Soldier dies

So enjoy your Freedom, your family and fun
But stop to remember where it all came from
Freedom is triumph over evil and lies
And it's paid for each time a Soldier dies

Note: Jim Willis at this writing is the State of Oregon, Director of Veteran's Affairs. Jim gave me verbal authorization to publish his poem in my book. I met him at a birthday party for a veteran at the McMinnville, Oregon American Legion/VFW Hall. Monique Godfrey, daughter-in-law of Ray Godfrey (an elder in the church that I pastor), wrote music to this poem and sang it that night. It was a great tribute to those who have given the ultimate sacrifice for the defense of freedom.

978-0-595-41175-7
0-595-41175-4

Printed in the United States
63327LVS00003B/56